ON DUTY

Escott Reid in September 1947. Photo courtesy of Public Archives of Canada.

ON DUTY

A Canadian at the
Making of the United Nations,
1945–1946

Escott Reid

McClelland and Stewart

Published in Canada by
McClelland and Stewart Limited
The Canadian Publishers
25 Hollinger Road
Toronto, Ontario
M4B 3G2

Canadian Cataloguing in Publication Data
Reid, Escott.
  On Duty.

Bibliography: p.
Includes index.
ISBN 0-7710-7442-5

1. United Nations—History. 2. Reid, Escott. 3. Diplomats—Canada—Biography. 4. Canada—Foreign relations—1945–1970.* I. Title.

JX1976.R44   354.1′03′09044   C83-098369-4

This book has been published with the help of a grant from the Social Science Federation of Canada, using funds provided by the Social Sciences and Humanities Research Council of Canada.

To Ruth, Patrick, Morna, and Timothy

Contents

Foreword

If Dean Acheson had not preempted the title "Present at the Creation," it would have fitted superbly the current memoir of Escott Reid. In fact, it might make a better fit for him than for Acheson. To quote further from the proverb Acheson used, "I would have given some useful hints for the better ordering of the universe." Unlike Acheson, Reid was a supporting actor whose useful hints were too frequently ignored. He was a leading but not the lead member of the Canadian delegation at the San Francisco Conference, at the Executive Committee of the Preparatory Commission, at the Preparatory Commission, and at the first session of the General Assembly of the United Nations. His nation was, as he frequently observes, a middle power on the scene with limited influence. He himself had an important but not always a final voice in Canadian contributions to the creation of the United Nations in the critical period from the spring of 1945 to the end of 1946.

This volume of letters, memoranda, and reflections comprises the third in a remarkable series of books which reveal the accomplishments and failures of a career in diplomacy, each distinct from the other both in method of presentation and in the roles played by the author. *Envoy to Nehru*, published in 1981, related his views of Canadian-Indian relations and Indian foreign policy in general from a perch as high commissioner to India in the mid-1950s. His first book dealt with the process of creation, namely the establishment of the North Atlantic Treaty from a Canadian perspective. *Time of Fear and Hope*, published in 1977, remains the most important history of the formation of NATO, written from the inside but with a historian's detachment. It was the reputation he won from this book that led to an invitation by the Center for NATO Studies at Kent State University in 1980 to participate in its first international conference on the Alliance. He provided a major address on that occasion, elaborating on the treaty as he understood it a generation earlier.

Unlike his role in NATO in 1948–49 as second-in-command of the Department of External Affairs in Ottawa and unlike his position in New Delhi six years later at the summit of his diplomatic career, Escott Reid in 1945 was in an early stage of his service. He had come from a quasi-academic background with the secretaryship of the Canadian Institute of International Affairs following his years at Oxford, and entered the foreign service only in 1939, at the relatively mature age of thirty-four. His late arrival and his wide experience with the private sector of international relations set him apart from most of his colleagues in the diplomatic life, and helped to account for an independence of spirit that obviously bothered his superiors from time to time. Reid was an outspoken man with a touch of fanaticism which he recognized and deplored—but only occasionally. Serenity is worth seeking, as he once wrote to his wife (p. 106) but not if it meant failing to speak out for a just cause. Although such a spirit must have made associates uncomfortable, his sense of morality and his quest for action in its behalf earned their respect.

The building of the United Nations was a task worthy of any diplomat's best efforts, and Escott Reid spared none of his. As he wrote his wife and children, his life was consumed by the problem of how to create a new league of nations that would make a third world war impossible. Reid threw himself into the job, at the cost of a long separation from his family, and at one point at the cost of his health. The driving force was a conviction that some form of effective international government must be secured to prevent the continuation of "international anarchy" (p. 11). When the news of the atomic bomb arrived in the midst of preparations for a General Assembly, the need became all the more imperative. The new weapon touched a vein of deep pessimism over the future of mankind—"vistas of Titanic glooms of chasmed fears"—as he put it in a letter to his wife on the day of Hiroshima. But despite flashes of despair, the record reveals a streak of optimism in his personality that made efforts to change the world before disaster overcame it worth all the aggravation and frustration that accompanied them. At the same time, the forty-year-old diplomat was burdened with a sense of guilt out of his awareness that unlike older and younger contemporaries, he was of an age that escaped military service in both world wars.

Before being plunged into United Nations matters Reid participated in the conference in Chicago in the fall of 1944 which resulted in the formation of the International Civil Aviation Organization. He was disappointed in the results of that conference since he had hoped that the new organization would have powers comparable to those of the Civil Aeronautics Board of the United States—the proposal which Canada had put before the conference.

A countermodel in this same period was the Dumbarton Oaks Conference, where four major powers gathered to provide the infrastructure of a charter for the United Nations. The Dumbarton Oaks proposals, begun in the spring of 1944 and announced on October 7, 1944, outlined the framework of the United Nations, which provided for a Security Council of eleven states with permanent seats and the right of veto to the four great powers, and later to France. A major current in his book is his opposition to the spirit of the "Four Policemen," implicit though not stated in the Dumbarton Oaks proposals. He objected to the wide extent of the veto power of the five permanent members of the Security Council. There were, he believed, powerful arguments for each of the great powers having the right to veto the imposition of sanctions even against itself but under the Dumbarton Oaks proposals the right of veto extended far beyond this point.

His "personal charter for world sanity" was his manifesto against the Dumbarton Oaks approach, and its theme runs through the memoir in almost every issue during the momentous months of 1945 and 1946. Escott Reid failed to win his department's approval to make his proposals the basis for the Canadian government's position on the Charter. The most he won was an anonymous publication in an obscure journal and applause from such friendly journalists as James Reston of the *New York Times*. The veto power remained an issue on which the permanent members of the Council would not yield and on which his own government would not take a stand.

Blame for the failure is widely distributed. First was the Soviet Union, which wished for a United Nations as weak as possible, followed by the United States, which for different reasons could not surrender the veto power. Much of his annoyance is reflected in his reaction to the behavior of the Canadian leadership—or lack of leadership. Reid felt strongly that the objectives of the "middle powers" such as Canada accorded with the general interest of nations more closely than those of the very large or the very small.

What concerned him most were the lost opportunities that such a weak position uncovered. As shown in the important Executive Committee of the Preparatory Commission for the first General Assembly meeting, a strong united Canadian stance would automatically make Canada one of the Big Five, given corresponding weakness of the French and Scandinavian delegations. Canada could have been the driving force in maintaining a proper balance, as Reid envisaged, among the General Assembly and the Security Council and secretary-general. Article 10 revealed the potential power of the General Assembly[1] (pp 128–29). Instead, Canada squandered the opportunity by deferring to the pressures of the major powers. He believes that Canada alienated some of the middle and smaller countries by not showing greater independence of the major powers and that this was one of the reasons for its defeat in the first elections to the Security Council.

Depressed though the author may have been by his encounters, his recounting of his trials is a blessing to the reader. Some of the most valuable and most interesting pages in this memoir deal with his sharp, pithy, and sometimes unfair observations of his colleagues and superiors in the Canadian delegation and elsewhere. Not surprisingly, a link may be made between those who support Reid's positions and those who are either indifferent or hostile to them. The great leaders lost their luster. Trygve Lie, the first secretary-general, (p. 140) and his own prime minister, Mackenzie King, emerge as "second-rate" (pp. 33–34). Both succumb to pressures from the great powers.

But his sharpest comments are reserved for Americans, particularly Edward Stettinius, secretary of state from October 1944

---

[1]Article 10 of the United Nations Charter, Functions and Powers. "The General Assembly may discuss any questions or any matters within the scope of the present Charter or relating to the powers and functions of any organs provided for in the present Charter, and, except as provided in Article 12, may make recommendations to the Members of the United Nations or to the Security Council or to both on any such questions or matters."

to June 1945 and then head of the American delegation to the
United Nations. Stettinius is both "ignorant" and "incompetent." At best he is pathetic as he constantly turns to an adviser
with cries for help (p. 25). Congressional delegates Senator Tom
Connally and Congressman Sol Bloom are characterized as
"overbearing and stupid." The only compensation for this unfortunate Democratic presence, according to the author, is that the
superior quality of Republicans Harold Stassen and Arthur Vandenberg (p. 42) should relieve the world of current fears of a future
Republican victory at the polls.

Inevitably, Reid's feelings of the moment color his percep-
tions of the people around him, as do the positions they take on
issues which concern him. One can identify the underside of his
happy Oxford memories—British class consciousness and snob-
bishness—in his description of the historian Charles K. Webster
as a "domineering professor who speaks like God Almighty to
Job" (p. 49). The issue at the moment was British pressure upon
Commonwealth countries to accept the Big Four positions on the
appointments of deputy secretaries-general (p. 40). But when a
few months later at the Executive Committee of the Preparatory
Commission Reid eloquently but singly supports postponement
of the first General Assembly until January 1946, he records that
Webster was impressed with his reasoning and congratulated him
on his speech. He includes Webster among those senior colleagues of "intellectual distinction, public spirit, and charm"
(pp. 86, 13) whom he worked with in 1945.

His Canadian colleagues receive the most extensive commen-
taries. They are also the most complex and hence the most con-
vincing. For example, Hume Wrong appears to have been an antagonist, much as he does in *Time of Fear and Hope*. He blames
Wrong for his inability to share responsibility or listen to advice
at the General Assembly. Yet there is an underlying respect for his
integrity and for the differing stance Wrong took on the meaning
of the United Nations itself. Despite these barriers between the
men Reid pays respect to a first-rate mind and to a friendship that
surmounted vital differences of opinion.

Equally balanced is his running reflection on the behavior of
the Soviet Union's spokesmen. He notes their suspiciousness,
their rigidity, their apparent readiness to sabotage proceedings at
anytime by walking out of the U.N. "Life with the Russians," he

observes, "is difficult, but life without them would be impossible" (p. 78). Their strong defense of the veto right made the Soviets a natural antagonist to the Canadian delegation. And still Reid could observe that their attitude was not too distant from the American and more defensible. The Soviet Union was in a minority in the United Nations, with major power resting with the United States and its allies. Once the Russians recognized that they could use the United Nations as a forum for opposition there was some relaxation but not much. Trouble derived from their lack of familiarity with English and French as well as from their fear of capitalist betrayal. The very idea of an international civil service was foreign to them. But as individuals they gradually warmed up and turned out to be not only among the most successful international lawyers but also congenial individuals.

In examining his own record he notes his special contributions. Probably his most notable combat was on behalf of clear and precise English prose in contrast to the language of the League or of the Dumbarton Oaks proposals which were the model for others. He failed but not without fighting the good fight. Reid seems to relish the obituary Sydney Gruson of the *New York Times* once suggested: "He died for English" (p. 121).

Less enjoyable was the losing battle, expressed with considerable bitterness, over the United States as the seat of the U.N. But there was a particular personal triumph as well. Reid took a strong stand on the importance of postponing the meeting of the General Assembly until the Preparatory Commission had completed detailed recommendations on all the organizational problems which would confront it so that the Assembly could concentrate on questions of substance (pp. 86–87). The larger powers wanted an early session of the Assembly that would do little more than show its face. He seems to have won his point at the Executive Committee session when he stood alone against the plan of having the General Assembly for two or three weeks in the fall of 1945 as simply an organizational meeting (p. 86). There is not much hyperbole in his statement that "I did more in a week in the Executive Committee to influence the future of the U.N. than the whole Canadian delegation will do in the four weeks of the Assembly."

The value of this important memoir, however, does not rest

on the specific accomplishments or the specific failures of the author. It may be found in part in the revelation of character and values displayed in the letters and broadsides of Escott Reid. With all his concerns for the moment and for the future, this burdened public servant recognized what mattered most. For a world to survive the international atomic age, organization was the only alternative to chaos. The United Nations was to be the expression it would take in 1945; four years later the Atlantic Alliance would be the means of preserving stability when the U.N. could not prevent the schism of East and West. As a middle-level official of a middle-level nation, Reid offers insights into the establishment of the United Nations which may not have been available to higher-level diplomats representing more powerful nations.

Lawrence S. Kaplan
Lyman L. Lemnitzer Center
  for NATO Studies
Kent State University

Preface

From late April 1945 to early February 1946 I worked full-time as an officer of the Canadian Department of External Affairs on the making of the United Nations. I served first at the United Nations Conference in San Francisco which approved a Charter based on the Dumbarton Oaks proposals of the four sponsoring powers (Britain, China, the Soviet Union, and the United States), and then at the three U.N. conferences in London: the fourteen-nation Executive Committee of the Preparatory Commission, the fifty-nation Preparatory Commission, and the first part of the first session of the General Assembly. Not many people participated in all four conferences. Of those who did few survive.

For all but three weeks of this nine-month period I was separated from my wife, Ruth. Extracts from my letters to her constitute the core of this book. All letters are to her unless otherwise noted. The letters are supplemented by official papers I wrote at the time and by explanatory memoranda.

My participation in the making of the United Nations was one of the three most interesting periods in my career in the Canadian foreign service which lasted from 1939 to 1962. I have written about the other two periods in my *Time of Fear and Hope: the Making of the North Atlantic Treaty, 1947–1949*, and in my *Envoy to Nehru*, which covers the years 1952 to 1957. This book thus completes a trilogy.

I have referred in this book to the memoirs of only a few other participants in the meetings on the United Nations in 1945 and 1946 and I have not made use of the many excellent books and articles by scholars on the making of the United Nations. To have done so would have taken a good deal of my time and my time is limited. I am seventy-eight and there are two or three more books I want to write before, with increasing age, the physical and psychological costs of writing books become too great.

The Canada Council gave me a grant towards my expenses in writing this book. The historical division and the Library of the Department of External Affairs in Ottawa helped me to locate documents and books. The Social Science Federation of Canada secured reports on the manuscript from two readers. Their suggestions for revision of the manuscript were most helpful. The book has been published with the help of a grant from the Social Science Federation of Canada, using funds provided by the Social Sciences and Humanities Research Council of Canada. Ernestine Hopkins typed and retyped the manuscript with skill and intelligence. To all these I am most grateful. And I owe a special debt of gratitude to Lawrence S. Kaplan for writing the foreword to this book.

In the first chapter of this book I state that from 1932 to 1969 I consistently worked too hard, played too little, and sacrificed my wife and children to my work. I dedicate this book to them in the hope that it may help to explain, though not to justify my conduct.

Ste. Cécile de Masham
Québec, May 1983

Chronology of Acts Leading to the Establishment of the United Nations

London Declaration of 12 June 1941

By all nations fighting Nazi Germany, announcing intentions to work together to establish a "world in which, relieved of the menace of aggression, all may enjoy economic and social security."

Atlantic Charter, 14 August 1941

Joint Anglo-American Declaration—final paragraph:
"They believe that all the nations of the world, for realistic as well as spiritual reasons, must come to the abandonment of the use of force. Since no future peace can be maintained if land, sea, or air armaments continue to be employed by nations which threaten, or may threaten, aggression outside of their frontiers, they believe, *pending the establishment of a wider and permanent system of general security*, that the disarmament of such nations is essential."

Declaration by United Nations, 1 January 1942

A joint declaration of common war aims, signed by the Big Four—U.S., USSR, U.K., China—and followed alphabetically by twenty-two nations (including India but not France), subscribing "to a common programme of purposes and principles embodied in the joint Declaration of the President of the United States of America and the Prime Minister of Great Britain and Northern Ireland, dated August 14, 1941, known as the Atlantic Charter."

Moscow Declaration of the Big Four on General Security, 30 October 1943

"4. That they recognize the necessity of establishing at the earliest practicable date a general international organization, based on the principle of the sovereign equality of all peace-loving states, and open to membership by all such states, large and small, for the maintenance of international peace and security."

Declaration of Teheran Conference—Stalin, Roosevelt, Churchill, 1 December 1943

"We shall seek the cooperation and active participation of nations large and small, whose peoples in heart and mind are dedicated as our own peoples, to the elimination of tyranny and slavery, oppression and intolerance. We will welcome them, as they may choose to come, into a world family of Democratic Nations."

Dumbarton Oaks Proposals of the Big Four for the Establishment of a General International Organization, 21 August–7 October 1944

"There should be established an international organization under the title of the United Nations, the Charter of which should contain provisions necessary to give effect to the proposals which follow."
Principal organs of the U.N.—General Assembly, Security Council, Economic and Social Council, International Court of Justice, and Secretariat—identified in conversations between U.S.A., U.K., and USSR, from 21 August to 28 September 1944 and between U.S.A., U.K., and China between 29 September and 7 October 1944.

Yalta Conference, 4–11 February 1945—Protocol of Proceedings

"I. *World Organization*
"It was decided that a United Nations Conference on the proposed world organization should be summoned for Wednesday, 25th April 1946, and should be held in the United States of America."
At Yalta the U.S., U.K., and USSR agreed to exclude the veto power of the permanent members from procedural matters and to apply U.N. trusteeship to existing League mandates, colonies to be detached from the enemy as a result of the war, and any other territory that might voluntarily be placed under trusteeship.

San Francisco Conference, 25 April–26 June 1945

Completed what Dumbarton Oaks had begun—issues of trusteeship and colonial territories, reaffirmed the veto power of the permanent members under the Yalta formula, but liberalized the powers of the General Assembly in Articles 10, 11, and 13 of Charter. Criticism by "middle powers," particularly Canada, resulted in Article 44 which provides that if a country not on the Security Council is called on to provide troops to enforce peace it shall be entitled to join in Security Council's discussions, and vote on use of its forces.

Executive Committee of Preparatory Commission, 16 August–27 October 1945

Recommendations of 14 states to the Preparatory Commission. The 143-page report contained recommendations on the agendas and rules of procedure of the Assembly, the Security Council, the Economic and Social Council, and the Trusteeship Council; on the organization of the Secretariat; on budgetary and financial arrangements; on the permanent headquarters of the U.N.; on the privileges, immunities, and facilities of the U.N.; and on the relations of the U.N. with the League of Nations.

Preparatory Commission, London, 24 November–23 December 1945

Recommendations of the member states of the U.N. to the principal organs of the U.N. The 150-page report consisted in the main of a revision of the report of the Executive Committee.

U.N. Charter comes into force, 10 October 1945—under Terms of Art. 110 of Charter.

First meeting of General Assembly, London, 10 January 1946.

1
Introduction

A leading Canadian historian who read an earlier version of this book said that I should include in the introduction "a brief personal biography that would explain to the readers just who you were in 1945 and how you got there." To write more than a superficial explanation is not easy, if only for the reason that I am removed by almost forty years from the person who wrote the letters in this book.

I can, in one sense, easily say who I was in 1945. I was forty years old, an Anglo-Saxon-Celtic Protestant, married with three children, aged nine, eleven, and fourteen, and I was first secretary at the Canadian embassy in Washington. Since joining the Canadian foreign service in January 1939 I had served in Washington from 1939 to 1941 and again in 1944 and 1945 and, in between, I had served in the Department of External Affairs in Ottawa. If I try to explain on a deeper level who I was in 1945 and how I got there, I have to go back to my upbringing. I was born in 1905, the youngest of five children, in a small town in southern Ontario where my father was the Anglican clergyman. After studying theology at St. Augustine's in Canterbury, my father had come to Canada in 1885 and had served in parishes in New Brunswick, British Columbia, Ontario, and northern New York State. In 1911, when I was six years old, he moved to Toronto where he had been a curate in the nineties, and I lived in Toronto from 1911 to 1927. Most of my father's parishioners in Toronto were poor and in those days the rectors of poor parishes had a very small income.

My father was a good man, a very good man, a devout Christian, compassionate, indeed something of a Christian socialist, not an intellectual, but with a theology liberal by the standards of those days. I have never heard anyone read the services in the Anglican prayer book more beautifully than he. I have sometimes been told that I have an English accent and that I must have acquired it at Oxford. My accent, however, was the same before Oxford as afterwards, and if my accent is English I probably acquired it by subconsciously modelling it on my father's because of my admiration for the beauty of his voice. My father maintained till his death his interest in what was happening in the world. In 1954, when my father was ninety-three, Walter Gordon and his wife, who had been staying with us in New Delhi, called on my parents. Walter Gordon wrote me: "I hope I am as interested in what is going on in the world when I am within thirty or forty years of your Father's age." I understand that, sometime in the first decade of the century, my father might have been appointed the rector of a well-to-do church in a prosperous small city in southern Ontario if he had not in his second sermon at the church—the sermon at the evening service—indicated his shock at what he had seen in the city since the morning service of the gap between the standards of living of the rich and of the poor. Certainly his career in the church suffered from his outspokeness. I did not realize until he was ninety-four that he brooded on this, and perhaps he had not brooded on it until then. I was staying with my parents in Toronto in the summer of 1955 when I was on home leave from India and I was about to leave the house to call on the bishop of Toronto, whose brother in India, also a bishop, was a friend, when my father took me aside and said, "If there is an opportunity could you say to the bishop how hurt I am that men much younger than I have been made canons and I haven't." If I have at times damaged my career by being too outspoken I come by the fault honestly.

Until I was sixteen and started working, I faithfully performed all the observances then expected of a rector's son. We had family prayers after our evening dinner when my father read the prayers and I one of the psalms for the day. On Sundays I went to church once, sometimes twice; during Lent I went to church on Wednesday evening; I went to Sunday school. When I became old enough to graduate from being a pupil at Sunday school to being a teacher, I escaped by taking on the job of administrative officer of the Sunday school, which consisted mainly in counting the collection. When my father gave one of his sermons which I had heard many times, I would open my prayer book and study the Latin at the beginning of each psalm, or the Elizabethan thirty-nine articles of religion of 1563, or the table of kindred and affinity, which interested me by stating among other things that a man might not marry his grandmother or his deceased wife's sister's daughter. I doubt whether I realized at the time that many of the thirty-nine articles were models for draftsmen at international conferences. When the authors wanted to leave no doubt about what they meant they used the fewest possible words: "The Bishop of Rome hath no jurisdiction in this Realm of England." When their object was to gloss over theological differences they were wordy and ambiguous.

My mother was intelligent, well read, animated, and full of nervous energy. I probably inherit my nervous energy from her. She had been brought up in comfort in Rosedale, Toronto. Her marriage plunged her into the genteel semi-poverty of a clergyman's family and she had her five children in the first ten years of marriage. She took refuge in books from the tribulations of the wife of a poor clergyman and there were always books in our living room—our own and borrowed from libraries. She was a sceptic about things temporal; she despised Winston Churchill because she felt that he enjoyed running the war, unlike one of her few heroes, Abraham Lincoln, who was torn by pity and sorrow for the sufferings of the Civil War. She refused to accept the adulation of the Old Testament partriarchs common among good Christians when she was young: she had a contempt for Isaac and Jacob and David. Because she was a clergyman's wife she hid any doubts she may have had about church doctrines. Once, however, when I was about twenty, I was standing beside her in church when the creed was being recited, and she said to me after the service, "You were silent at just the same passages my father would never recite." Early in 1945 a close friend and contemporary of my mother died. In a letter to me my mother gave a description of her. I wrote back, "Your description of her sounds so much like yourself, 'lovely to look at, and very intellectual and charming, with a curious fibre of cynicism in her gentle, aristocratic character.' "

My father was proud of what he called his yeoman farmer ancestors in England and Ireland. My mother was likewise proud of her ancestors. She worshipped her father, Edmund Meredith. I never knew him but I think he must have been very intelligent and the possessor of much Irish charm. He was descended from a long line of southern Irish Protestant lawyers, clergy, and doctors who had studied at Trinity College, Dublin. He came to Canada in

1842, was appointed unpaid principal of McGill University, Montreal, in 1846 at the age of twenty-nine, and served until 1849. He was a member of the Canadian civil service for thirty-one years, from 1847 to 1878. From 1948 to 1952, when I was deputy undersecretary of state for external affairs, I had an office in the East Block of the Parliament Buildings in Ottawa, which I afterwards discovered was the office my grandfather had occupied in 1867 at the time of Confederation, when he was assistant secretary of state for the provinces.

My mother's mother was descended from two of the founding families of Toronto (then York), the Jarvises, and the Powells. They were United Empire Loyalists and members of the Family Compact which dominated the government of Ontario (then Upper Canada) until the rebellion of 1837, led by William Lyon Mackenzie—the grandfather of W. L. Mackenzie King, prime minister of Canada for more than twenty years. My mother's maternal grandfather, a Jarvis, was sheriff in Toronto at the time of the rebellion and, according to one historian, William Kilbourn, was responsible for breaking the back of the rebellion in Upper Canada. He headed a sheriff's picket of twenty-seven men which, at the outskirts of Toronto at Carlton and Yonge Streets, met a group of hundreds of rebels moving south to seize Toronto. Both sides fired a volley and both sides then fled—all except the sheriff. By fleeing the rebels lost their last chance to seize Toronto. The sheriff's father, Stephen, had likewise fought rebels but not so successfully. He was a farmer's son from Danbury, Connecticut. In the American War for Independence he fought in the loyalist forces, first as a sergeant in the Queen's Rangers, and then as a lieutenant in the 17th Light Dragoons. After the success of the Revolution he left the United States for Canada. The paternal grandfather of the sheriff's wife, a Powell, was born in Boston, migrated to Montreal in 1779, and became a judge of the Court of King's Bench in Upper Canada in 1794 and chief justice of Upper Canada in 1816.

I went to public school and high school in Toronto. I was at high school from 1917 to 1921. I now find it hard to believe that in the spring of 1918, when I was thirteen, I assumed that the war would last until it was time for me to enlist at the age of seventeen or eighteen. I intended to take an officers' training course at high school since I was told that if I did I would be given the rank of sergeant when I enlisted. Between high school and university I worked for two years as a clerk in the audit department of the Ontario government in order to save money to go to university, and I took my senior matriculation by attending night high school with the result that when I was sixteen, seventeen, and eighteen I worked too hard and played too little. When I was at university in Toronto and Oxford from 1923 to 1930 I did not again fall into this error, nor when I was investigating Canadian political parties from 1930 to 1932. But from 1932, when I became national secretary of the Canadian Institute of International Affairs, to 1969, when I retired from the principalship of Glendon College, I consistently worked too hard and played too little and sacrificed my wife and children to my work. In part this arose from my obsession from 1933 on with the danger of a second world war, and from 1943 on with the danger of a third world war. I was determined from 1943 on that the Canadian government should do its utmost to reduce the chances of a third world war breaking out, and that I should do my utmost to persuade the Canadian government to do its utmost. The result was that I worked myself to the point of nervous exhaustion at the Chicago conference on international civil aviation in November 1944, at the Preparatory Commission of the United Nations in London in December 1945, in the arguments over the Baruch proposals in the U.N. Atomic Energy Commission in December 1946, in the negotiation of the North Atlantic Treaty in 1948 and 1949, in the crises in the first nine months of the Korean War in 1950 and 1951 when General Douglas MacArthur seemed determined to precipitate war with China and perhaps the Soviet Union, and in trying to persuade Nehru in November 1956 to oppose publicly the Soviet Union's suppression of the Hungarian Revolution.

By the time I entered the University of Toronto (Trinity College) in 1923 I was a socialist, a Canadian nationalist, and a fervent believer in the League of Nations. In my first year at the university I was a member of a group of a dozen or so students who tried to establish a branch of the socialistic League for Industrial Democracy, and I was active in the Student Christian Movement, which then included most of the leading radical students of Protestant Christian upbringing. I took a leading part in college and university debates. I was first with first-class honours in my four years in the honours course in political science. All this marked me out as a potential Rhodes scholar. But one of the requirements for a Rhodes scholarship was that the applicant have physical vigour demonstrated by participation in athletics or in other ways. I was no good at athletics so I demonstrated my physical vigour in the summer of 1926 by working as a labourer on a railway extra gang during the day, and teaching the other labourers at night as a Frontier College instructor. I was awarded a Rhodes scholarship that autumn.

From 1927 to 1930 I was at Christ Church, Oxford. I supplemented my income from the Rhodes Trust with two scholarships, which I won at Oxford, and, for the first time in my life, I had money for a few luxuries—good clothes, books, and travel. I loved Oxford and London and the English countryside. I had many British friends and acquaintances. I enjoyed life at Oxford. I debated in the Oxford Union, was elected secretary of the Union, and was defeated twice for the presidency. I may have been the first Canadian to stand for the presidency of the Union. I was treasurer of the university Labour Club and president of the English Club. The committee of the English Club when I was president included Stephen Spender and Elizabeth Harman (later Elizabeth Longford), who had the well-deserved reputation of being the most distinguished intellectual among the women undergraduates. The membership fee for the club was low but we had hundreds of members and the revenue from fees was sufficient to pay for excellent dinners at which the committee entertained itself and the speaker of the evening.

I do not think that my general approach to domestic policy or foreign policy changed much while I was at Oxford. This was the period before Hitler and the depression began only in my final year. It was, up to the autumn of 1929, a period of great hope for continued economic and social progress and for international cooperation. I was at Geneva during the League of Nations Assembly in 1929, the golden year of Ramsay Macdonald, Aristide Briand, and Gustav Stresemann. In a sense we were still living in the last decades of the nineteenth century, when people in the western world believed that everything was getting better and better and would continue to get better and better.

I think that the principal effect which my years at Oxford had on me was that they gave me more self-confidence. I sharpened my ability to suck the marrow out of books quickly, to write essays

quickly and clearly, and to speak in public persuasively and sometimes with wit. I acquired more social poise. I became aware that
the social-democratic views I professed, which were in Canada
held by few, were in Britain the conventional wisdom of probably
more than half the intelligentsia. I won the coveted award of a first
class in my final examinations in Modern Greats (philosophy,
politics, and economics). I think that Hume Wrong and Douglas
LePan were the only contemporaries of mine in the External Affairs service to have been awarded a first class at Oxford or its
equivalent. All this no doubt accentuated my tendency to intellectual and moral arrogance.

My love of England was not blind. I was shocked by the physical differences in England between the upper classes and the
working class, the result of generations of the working class having bad food and bad housing. As with virtually all Canadian
Rhodes scholars in the years between the two world wars, my stay
in Oxford made me even more of a Canadian nationalist, partly, I
suppose, because I could see nothing in the British I knew to justify Britain having a superior status to Canada.

At a lecture on Kant by the Master of Balliol, A. D. Lindsay, I
saw a remarkably beautiful and vivacious girl. I found out that
she was Ruth Herriot, from Winnipeg, who was studying at St.
Hugh's College. We were married a few months after we returned
to Canada from Oxford. She has influenced me more than anyone
else. I shall not myself attempt to characterize her. I shall instead
quote what my mother wrote me about her early in 1946, after we
had been married fifteen years. In one letter she said: "Ruth often
reminds me of my mother in her gaiety, endurance and common
sense." And in another letter: "She would give her life for you or
any one of the children, and give it quite simply, without fuss, if
she could save one of you. I admire Ruth's endurance and, under
her sophistication, her simplicity of heart. Also I take pleasure in
her extra long lashes, her easy adjustment to queer situations and
her charm of manner."

By the time I left Oxford in 1930 the depression had deepened
and jobs were scarce, but I managed to secure a Rockefeller Foundation fellowship in the social sciences. I never did complete the
doctoral thesis on Canadian political parties on which I was
working, since I became overwhelmed by the statistics I compiled
on voting patterns in Canadian federal elections. I did, however,

publish articles in learned periodicals, and I am happy that some of these articles have stood the test of time and that university students today are still advised to read them. My failure in the early thirties to write the book I should have written made me determined when I retired to complete any book I started on. I have now completed four. I agree with the narrator in one of Anthony Powell's novels: "Writing may not be enjoyable, its discontinuance can be worse. . . ."

In the summer of 1932, just before my fellowship from the Rockefeller Foundation was about to expire and I did not know what work I could get, I was offered the post of national secretary of the Canadian Institute of International Affairs (C.I.I.A.). I accepted the offer. I was instructed to open an office in Toronto, to assist the branches of the Institute to secure speakers, to establish new branches, and to help organize two unofficial conferences which were to be held in Canada in 1933—the Institute of Pacific Relations Conference in Banff and the British Commonwealth Relations Conference in Toronto. Two weeks after I had accepted the post with the C.I.I.A. I received an invitation from W. Y. Elliott to join the Department of Government at Harvard, where I had spent a few months in the winter of 1931–32. If the invitation from Harvard had arrived earlier, and it might have if it had not been misdirected, I might have accepted it rather than the post in the C.I.I.A. I often speculate on how this might have affected my life. Would I have made a career at Harvard as a political scientist or, after Roosevelt came to power, would I have jumped at an opportunity to leave Harvard to join a New Deal agency in Washington? If I had joined a New Deal agency, might I have become a member of a left-wing discussion group used by the Soviet government as a recruiting ground for agents? Certainly I had by the mid-thirties decided, like most liberals and social democrats, including Jawaharlal Nehru, that if, as then seemed possible, the choice before us became limited to fascism or communism, I would choose communism.

There were two great advantages to me of the posts I held in the thirties. The first was that they made it necessary for me to travel across Canada from coast to coast about half a dozen times visiting all the principal cities; from 1930 to 1932 I was collecting material on the development of Canadian political parties; from 1932 to 1938 I was visiting the branches of the Canadian Institute of International Affairs. I talked to leading Canadians, especially in universities and newspapers, and made friends with many of them: Frank Underhill, J. W. Dafoe, Edgar Tarr, J. M. Macdonnell, Frank Scott, Paul Martin, Hume Blake, Norman MacKenzie, Brooke Claxton, George Ferguson, John Bird, Ralegh Parkin, Henry Angus, T. W. L. MacDermot, King Gordon, Graham Spry, Eugene Forsey, Loring Christie, and many others.

The second advantage to me of my posts in the thirties was that I lived for almost all the time in Toronto, which in the thirties was the centre of left-wing intellectual activity in Canada. I was a member of the small closely knit group of friends and acquaintances centred at the University of Toronto who worked together in some or all of the following organizations: the Canadian Institute of International Affairs, the League of Nations Society, the Canadian Political Science Association, the *Canadian Forum*, the League for Social Reconstruction founded in 1932 (the Canadian counterpart of the British Fabian Society), and the Cooperative Commonwealth Federation, the social-democratic party likewise founded in 1932. In the thirties I was a member of the Left Book Club and an avid reader of its books, especially those by H. N. Brailsford, G. D. H. Cole, Harold Laski, Arthur Koestler, Leonard Woolf, John Strachey, and Vigilantes. My approach to international affairs in the first half of the thirties was much the same as that of most of the members of the Left Book Club, indeed of most liberals and social democrats in Britain, the United States, and Canada. We believed that the only way to prevent a second world war was to create an effective system of collective security under which the strengthening of the provisions in the covenant of the League of Nations for enforcing sanctions against an aggressor state would be accompanied by revision of the Versailles peace treaty of 1919, which Maynard Keynes had taught us was an iniquitous Carthaginian peace, and by international agreements on access to raw materials and markets. When by the mid-thirties it seemed that there was little or no chance of carrying out such a programme and that a second world war was inevitable, I advocated that Canada should stay out of that war. Like almost all the senior members of the Department of External Affairs in Ottawa at the time—O. D. Skelton, Loring Christie, Hugh Keenleyside, Scott Macdonald, and probably Laurent Beaudry—and most of the leading members of the League for Social Reconstruction, I believed that there was a balance of forces in Europe and that it was up to the Europeans to settle their own affairs. We overestimated the strength of the French army and underestimated the strength of the German army. It was not until France fell in June 1940 that I became convinced that Canada had to participate fully in the war.

When I joined the Department of External Affairs in January 1939 I was given the rank of second secretary. Other officers about my age had been in the Department for half a dozen years and, because no promotions were made during the depression, they were still third secretaries. I was parachuted into the Department over their heads and my appointment was by order-in-council not by examination. This, and the fact that I had held an influential post for six years before joining the Department and had written extensively on Canadian foreign policy in learned periodicals and popular magazines, gave me a feeling that persisted throughout my career in the foreign service, that I was not a professional diplomat. I certainly did not feel committed to stay in the Canadian foreign service until I reached the retirement age of sixty-five. After the war ended I frequently toyed with the idea of resigning and I finally did in 1962 at the age of fifty-seven.

There were four events in my first five years in the Canadian foreign service, the years 1939 to 1943, which left a lasting imprint on my mind. The first was Canadian policy before the outbreak of the war on the admission to Canada of German and Austrian Jews. After two months at the Canadian legation in Washington I wrote in March 1939 to my wife, who had had to remain in Toronto until I succeeded in finding a house in Washington:

> A terribly sad, good-looking and charming Jew came in to see me this morning about getting his parents out of Vienna. They are too frightened even to go to the U.S. consulate. His father has already been attacked on the street by some young hooligans. Every time one of them comes in it leaves me shaken and ashamed of Canada. I can't see any reason why we can't let these old people in when they are not going to work and their children in the States are willing and able to support them. It's like being a bystander at an especially cruel and long-drawn-out murder.

Then in June 1940 I watched from Washington, in horrified

fascination, the spectacle of a proud great power, powerless to prevent the clear and present threat to its independence, which would have resulted after the fall of France from a German occupation of the British Isles.

In January 1942, after Pearl Harbor, when I was in the Department of External Affairs in Ottawa, I attended a meeting to discuss what, if anything, should be done about the Japanese-Canadians in British Columbia. The civil servants were united in advocating that the Japanese-Canadians not be interned. The members of a delegation of politicians from British Columbia were unanimous that they be expelled from the province and interned. They spoke of the Japanese-Canadians in the way the Nazis would have spoken about Jewish-Germans. When they spoke I felt in that committee room the physical presence of evil. The politicians won.

In August 1943, when I learned of the bombing of Hamburg, I wrote to my mother:

Hamburg is the culminating horror. My hands feel unclean simply because I am a citizen of an allied government. War is the dirtiest of all businesses and perhaps the misery of Hamburg will curtail the misery of the more innocent women and children of France, the Netherlands, Norway and the Jews. I hope we can lay that flattering unction to our souls. It looks as if the war will end in a nightmare of aerial devastation of Germany. But it also looks as if the war will end sooner than we had dared hope.

By 1943 I had come to the conclusion that if we were to preserve peace after the war there had to be an end to the international anarchy, which was in my opinion the cause of the two world wars. In its place there had to be created a system of international government consisting of strong international functional agencies and a strong central organization, a strengthened League of Nations. I participated in the conference in Chicago in November and December 1944, which resulted in the establishment of one of the functional agencies, the International Civil Aviation Organization; but I.C.A.O. was not the strong agency I had hoped and worked for. I wanted a regulatory agency which would be the international equivalent of the Civil Aeronautics Board of the United States. I believed that Soviet membership in the functional international agencies was desirable, provided that the price of Soviet membership was not too great a weakening of the powers of the agency, but that Soviet membership was not essential. The World Bank, the International Monetary Fund, the Food and Agriculture Organization, the International Labor Organization, UNESCO, and I.C.A.O., could get along without the Soviet Union. But Soviet membership in the new United Nations was essential. Our task was to create the strongest possible United Nations consistent with Soviet membership.

I was in the middle of the Atlantic on 7 August 1945 en route from Ottawa to London when I learned that an atomic bomb had been dropped on Hiroshima. I wrote that day to my wife:

> I am in despair today about the kind of world our children are going to live in. I have hoped against hope until today that the atomic bomb would not be discovered. Now all the vistas of titanic glooms of chasmed fears open up. . . . I just haven't enough faith in man or god to believe that we have enough time or intelligence or goodwill to reach the goal of world government before we obliterate civilization in another war. But there's nothing to do except to live *as if* it were possible, and to try one's best to make it possible.

In this book I discuss some of the might-have-beens of the years 1945 and 1946. I believe that some of the mistakes made in those years could have been avoided and we would have created a better United Nations than we did. What Sir Percival Spear wrote in the introduction to his Oxford history of modern India applies, I believe, to the history of the making of the United Nations:

> During this period of Indian history it is specially necessary to avoid the mistake of interpreting the past in terms of the future. What has occurred in time cannot be undone, but it does not necessarily follow that nothing else could have happened, or that the actual course of events was the only possible or even probable outcome of the interplay of historical forces and personalities.[1]

One of the themes in this book is the erosion of the wartime alliance between the western world and the Soviet world, which took place in 1945, an erosion which led to what I called, in a memorandum in February 1946, a schism between the two worlds.

The schism widened in the next year and a half and by the summer of 1947 I was advocating the creation of an alliance against the Soviet Union. I tell the story of the creation of that alliance and of the part I played in its creation in my *Time of Fear and Hope: the Making of the North Atlantic Treaty.*

I refer frequently in this book to the four most influential officers in the Canadian foreign service in 1945 and 1946: Norman Robertson, Hume Wrong, Lester Pearson, and Dana Wilgress. Robertson was then undersecretary of state for external affairs, the senior officer in the Department in Ottawa and Wrong was his second-in-command. Pearson was ambassador in Washington and Wilgress, ambassador to the Soviet Union. I count myself fortunate that I had the opportunity to work with senior colleagues of such intellectual distinction, public spirit, and charm. I was fortunate also in the colleagues in other delegations with whom I worked, notably: Philip Noel-Baker, Gladwyn Jebb, and C. K. Webster of Great Britain; Adlai Stevenson, Andrew Cordier, and Benjamin Gerig of the United States; Herman van Roijen and Adrian Pelt of the Netherlands; Cyro de Freitas-Valle of Brazil; and, in particular, Paul Hasluck and Kenneth Bailey of Australia. I have in the explanatory memoranda in this book quoted extensively from Hasluck's perceptive writings.

I was an admirer and friend of Robertson, Wrong, Pearson, and Wilgress. They were all older than I: Robertson by only a year, Wrong by ten years, Pearson by eight, and Wilgress by twelve. At the time of the San Francisco Conference I was forty, Robertson forty-one, Wrong fifty, Pearson forty-eight, and Wilgress fifty-two.

Of the four, the one I was fondest of and the one with whom I was most in agreement was the oldest, Wilgress, and indeed I cannot recall any issue concerning the United Nations on which we differed in 1945 and 1946 or subsequently. One incident in New York in December 1946 illustrates how closely our instinctive reactions to these issues coincided. We both wanted Canada to oppose Bernard Baruch's efforts to bulldoze his proposals through the U.N. Atomic Energy Commission before they had been adequately examined. We were sitting behind General Andrew McNaughton, the Canadian delegate, when he gave a speech before the Commission on 20 December accepting a compromise.

As he spoke we unconsciously kept pushing our chairs farther and farther back from him in dislike of his speech, separating ourselves from what he was saying.

My association with Pearson on U.N. issues went back to 1944 when I was serving under him at the Canadian embassy in Washington and we were reporting to Ottawa on United States views on the future U.N. and on the Dumbarton Oaks Conference, and were making recommendations to Ottawa on Canadian policy. I cannot recall any issue on which we disagreed except for a relatively minor one at the San Francisco Conference (see my letter of 10 May 1945, p. 36 below) and his concurrence in McNaughton's recommendation to him that we agree to the compromise of 20 December 1946 on the Baruch proposals. I shared with Pearson in 1944 and 1945 hopes for the United Nations which Wrong considered utopian and I later shared similar utopian hopes with Pearson from 1947 to 1949 for the North Atlantic alliance which Wrong dismissed as unrealistic. Our hope was that the alliance would provide the basis for a North Atlantic community which would in time evolve into a federation.

Robertson was intellectually superior to Wilgress and Pearson, and was close to being Wrong's equal in intellect. He had great confidence in himself. In 1941, at the age of only thirty-seven, he was appointed head of the Department of External Affairs. Wrong and Pearson were older and senior to him in the service and they both thought their claim to the top post was better than his. Knowing this he invited them to come to Ottawa to work with him. A lesser man would have feared that their presence in Ottawa would weaken his position. Lesser men than Wrong and Pearson would have found some excuse for not serving under a man whose post they thought they should have had. Robertson was less willing than Pearson to consider unorthodox views about the U.N. and later the North Atlantic alliance, but more willing than Wrong. As I said to him in a letter in 1958 expressing my delight in his becoming for the second time the undersecretary for external affairs, he had a "creative imagination and well-stocked mind and . . . [a] habit of applying a disciplined scepticism to the old orthodoxies of international politics." A disciplined scepticism about old orthodoxies could sometimes lead him to conclusions not very different from those which Pearson and I might reach through utopianism. This had been the case when I served with Robertson on an interdepartmental committee on civil aviation in Ottawa in 1943 and 1944. On that committee, Robertson supported proposals for the establishment of an international civil aeronautics board which the United States administration certainly considered utopian.

I had only one difference of opinion with Wrong at the San Francisco Conference. That was during the crisis at the beginning of June over the veto. My view was that once we were convinced that the Soviet Union was not bluffing when it stated that it would refuse to join the U.N. if such-and-such a provision were in the Charter, or not in, we had to give in. Otherwise there would be no U.N. and we would have precipitated the formation of two rival alliances. I considered at the time that Wrong was much too ready to contemplate the immediate formation of these alliances. (See my letter of 6 June 1945, p. 56–59 below.)

I did not realize until Wrong came to London for the first session of the General Assembly in January 1946 the extent of our disagreements on the tactics we should follow in the Assembly. I wanted the Canadian delegation to oppose the very bad nominations the great powers had made for chairmen of committees, to oppose the Soviet attempts to get around the rules for secret ballots on elections, and to vote for the best candidates for the Economic and Social Council, regardless of the great-power slates. Wrong feared that to do these things would lessen our chances of being elected to the Security Council and the Economic and Social Council. He had his way and we failed to be elected to the Security Council. I believed at the time, and continue to believe, that if we had made the public demonstrations of independence of the great powers which I had recommended, we would probably have been elected. (See my letters of 13, 18, and 20 January 1946, pp. 136 and 137–39 below.)

It was not until the end of February 1946, when I read Wrong's draft memorandum giving his impressions of the General Assembly, that I realized that our disagreements about the U.N. went deeper than tactics. In the concluding sentence of his memorandum, Wrong stated that the question whether the establishment of the U.N. had in fact furthered the maintenance of international peace and security was an "open" one. I commented that in order to say this he "must be able to argue that the present situation would be no worse if the United Nations had not been established. . . . So far as I can judge, the quarrels [between the Soviet Union and the western powers] would have gone on anyway, and the existence of the United Nations has not made them worse. On the other hand the existence of the United Nations has already done some good and may do much more good in matters not directly related to their quarrels." (See my memorandum to Wrong of 25 February 1946, pp. 159–61).

The principal disagreements which I had with Hume Wrong were over two subjects on which I have written books: the making of the United Nations and the making of the North Atlantic Treaty. On most other aspects of Canadian foreign policy we were in substantial agreement. I admired Wrong greatly—his intellect, his trenchant style, his contempt for second-rate minds and slipshod writing. We were neighbours in the Gatineau hills north of Ottawa. His summer cottage and our farm were only about a mile apart. We never allowed our disagreements over policy to interfere with our friendship.

I had hoped that he would become undersecretary in Ottawa three or four years before he did. When he did become undersecretary in 1953 I wrote him a long letter suggesting various ways by which he might lighten the heavy burden of the office. At the end of my letter I said:

> I conclude with a prescription on how to keep sane with a big job. I think it may amuse you. It is an account which Jim Macdonnell gave me many years ago of Lothian's answer to a question about how Lloyd George carried his burden during the first world war: "You must know that Lloyd George had a theory that when a man had a big job either it got on top of him or he got on top of it. Pursuant to this, Lloyd George never tried to do what would be called a big day's work. He got up at a reasonable hour, had his breakfast leisurely, despatched business during the morning, always had a rest during the afternoon, never looked at documents at night though he might have business discussions during the evening, went to bed at a reasonable hour, took a good week-end, and would pull up in the middle of a week and go off for a day or two if he found himself getting below par." All best wishes for success in achieving leisurely breakfasts, afternoon rests and good week-ends.

Alas, Wrong became ill almost immediately after taking over the post of undersecretary and died a few months later.

One of my most pleasant memories is staying with Hume and Joyce Wrong at the Canadian embassy in Washington in September 1952 when Ruth, our daughter Morna, and I were on our way from Ottawa to Delhi to take up my post as high commissioner. And when I sent Hume the account of the visit which the three of us made to villages in India shortly after our arrival, he wrote me: "What a change you are having from the East Block [of the Parliament Buildings in Ottawa]! I think it a good thing to undertake a completely different sort of life from time to time and this you have done." Perhaps he wished he had had such an opportunity.

2

My "personal charter for world sanity"

Almost a quarter century after the San Francisco Conference, James Reston, who had covered the Conference for the *New York Times*, referred in his *Times* column to the "personal charter for world sanity" which I had brought to San Francisco.[1] This "personal charter" was a revision and expansion of the Dumbarton Oaks proposals preceded by a commentary. I had written this in the hope that the Department of External Affairs might use it as the basis for a document which would be published by the Canadian government three or four months before the San Francisco Conference and circulated to the governments which would be attending the Conference. The Department turned this suggestion down but gave me permission to have my draft charter published anonymously. It was published as a forty-page printed pamphlet by the Free World Research Bureau under the title "The Constitution of the United Nations," and it was circulated to the delegates to the Conference on 2 May 1945. At almost the same time the magazine *Free World* published the preamble and five chapters of my charter in its May issue. *Free World*, then in its ninth year, was published monthly in New York in eight languages. Its international editor was Louis Dolivet. The five chapters which it published were those on the rights of every man, the purposes of the United Nations, the Secretariat, pacific settlement of international disputes, and non-self-governing territories.

In my letter of 24 January 1945 to the Department of External Affairs enclosing a first draft of my charter I said:

The Chicago [International Civil] Aviation Conference demonstrated that the influence of a delegation at an international conference called to draw up an international instrument is greatly increased if, before the conference opens, the

state which the delegation represents publishes a well
worked-out complete draft of the international instrument.
Unless there are competing drafts, equally well worked-out
and complete, the chances are good that that state's draft will
be taken as the basis of discussion at the conference. [This
was what had happened at the Chicago Conference to the
Canadian draft of an agreement.] The draft proposals agreed
to at Dumbarton Oaks are neither complete nor in treaty
form. The great powers may complete them and put them in
treaty form before the general United Nations conference
meets. In that event the great power draft will be the basis of
discussion at the conference. Even then, however, a competing draft will exert a considerable measure of influence. The
influence will be particularly great if the new great power
draft has the faults of the Dumbarton Oaks draft—bad
draftsmanship, clumsy language, a complete lack of popular
appeal. Granting that it may not be possible to make large
changes in the structure of the Dumbarton Oaks proposals, it
may well be possible to make comparatively minor improvements in it at a hundred points and the result of a
hundred such minor improvements may be a hundred per
cent improvement in the proposals as a whole. The chances
of making a hundred minor improvements would be substantially increased if all the improvements were included in
a new draft published before the conference meets than if they
were moved one by one in committee at the conference. Conferences quickly get tired and when they get tired they tend to
reject amendments no matter how sound they are.

I am particulary proud of two sections in my draft charter.
One had to do with the veto rights of the permanent members of
the Security Council, the other with a declaration of human
rights. The section on the right of a permanent member to veto the
imposition of sanctions against itself foreshadowed the creation
of the North Atlantic alliance four years later.

If a situation should arise in which four great powers, and a
substantial number of the other powers, would be willing to
vote to impose sanctions against the fifth great power, but for
this provision . . . , those powers will be ready to declare
war against it. By imposing its veto the great power bent on

ORGANIZATION OF THE UNITED NATIONS

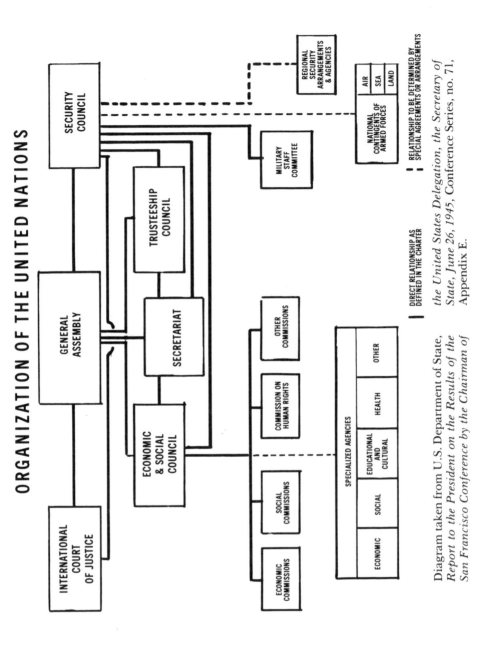

Diagram taken from U.S. Department of State, *Report to the President on the Results of the San Francisco Conference by the Chairman of the United States Delegation, the Secretary of State, June 26, 1945,* Conference Series, no. 71, Appendix E.

aggression will save itself from sanctions but not from war. If, in the unhappy event that a great power should in future act in such a way as to convince the other great powers that it is determined to dominate the world by force, the only way to prevent a world war from breaking out will be for the other great powers to form immediately an alliance against that power and to declare that the moment it commits aggression they will wage total war against it with their combined forces on land, on sea and in the air until it surrenders unconditionally. That declaration may bring the state which is planning aggression to its senses and so prevent the war from breaking out. The draft [Charter] does not prevent the peace-loving states from forming such an alliance against a war-minded state. Indeed by its provisions and by the machinery it creates it facilitates the formation of the alliance. A great power charged with aggression or with threatening aggression will immediately be brought to the bar of the Security Council which will examine the charges against it. If the examination shows that the great power against which the charges have been brought is in fact a menace to world peace, the other states which are members of the Council will, if their governments and peoples have not forgotten the lessons of the thirties, draw together in self-protection and, before they pronounce sentence of guilt, they will have forged an alliance against the guilty state.

So far as I know, my pamphlet sank without a trace when circulated to the delegates at San Francisco. The first chapter of my draft charter, "The rights of every man," may, however, have had some influence in the discussions in the U.N. on a declaration and convention of human rights, particularly since I took advantage of an opportunity early in 1947 to resurrect my proposals. Pearson, then undersecretary of state for External Affairs, called me in to see him on 23 February 1947. He said that the minister, Louis St. Laurent, was to give a speech the next day to the Montreal branch of the United Nations Association at which Eleanor Roosevelt, the chairman of the U.N. Commission on Human Rights, was to be present. The speech was to be on human rights. Unfortunately, by some inexplicable error, no speech had been prepared for St. Laurent. I therefore would have to write the speech and have it ready the next morning. He apologized for

giving me this difficult assignment. There was, he said, not time
for me to consider the kind of speech St. Laurent would like to
give. I should write the speech which I would give if I were the
principal speaker at the meeting. I did so. Among the passages I
included in the speech and which St. Laurent used were the
following:

> The Commission on Human Rights of the Economic and
> Social Council of the United Nations . . . entrusted to its
> Chairman, Mrs. Roosevelt, together with the vice-president
> . . . and the rapporteur . . . the task of preparing a tenta-
> tive draft of an international bill of human rights. . . . Mrs.
> Roosevelt and her colleagues will have at their disposal a
> number of draft declarations on human rights already pre-
> pared by distinguished sociologists and statesmen of several
> countries. I shall refer only to two of them. One was prepared
> approximately three years ago by a committee of "The Amer-
> ican Law Institute" on which sat Dr. P. E. Corbett, formerly
> of McGill, and Mr. C. W. Jenks, legal adviser of the Interna-
> tional Labour Organization, now a Montrealer. The other
> one appeared in the magazine "Free World" nearly two years
> ago. "Free World" patterned its draft on that of "The Ameri-
> can Law Institute" and made certain additions. I mention
> these two drafts because they both assert in their preambles
> principles that are basic. Here is how "Free World" expresses
> these principles. The first:
>
>> The individual man, woman and child is the corner-
>> stone of culture and civilization. He is the subject, the
>> foundation, the end of the social order. Upon his dig-
>> nity, his liberty, his inviolability depend the welfare of
>> the people, the safety of the State and the peace of the
>> world.
>
> The second one is expressed thus:
>
>> In society complete freedom cannot be attained. An in-
>> dividual possesses many rights but he may not exercise
>> any of them in a way which will destroy the rights of
>> others. No right exists in isolation from the other rights.
>> The liberties of one individual are limited by the liber-
>> ties of others and by the just requirements of the demo-
>> cratic state. The preservation of the freedom of the indi-
>> vidual requires not only that his rights be respected,

preserved and defended but also that he respect, preserve and defend the rights of others by fulfilling his duties as a member of society.

The third principle is expressed thus:

The state exists to serve the individual. He does not exist to serve the state. The state exists to promote conditions under which he can be most free.[2]

3

The San Francisco Conference

25 April–26 June 1945

I have never been able to understand how anyone who was at the San Francisco Conference could have had high hopes if he had known what was going on there and what was happening at the same time to the relations between the Soviet world and the western world in Europe. Yet some eminent and intelligent participants in that Conference have repeatedly said that they had high hopes. Lester Pearson, afterwards foreign minister and prime minister of Canada, was one of them.

I remember that towards the end of the Conference a number of us in the Canadian delegation were talking in the sitting room of the acting head of the delegation, Norman Robertson, about the results of the Conference. We bemoaned the errors the Conference had committed and the weaknesses in the Charter. We expressed our deep pessimism about the future of the United Nations. Norman Robertson, after listening to this litany of woe, commented that we must be careful not to talk that way outside our own group; people in general had high hopes for the U.N. and we must not do anything to undermine their hopes.

One of the principal weaknesses we saw in the Charter was the extent of the right of veto given to each of the five permanent members of the Security Council. There were powerful arguments for each of the great powers having the right to veto the imposition of sanctions even against itself, but the veto extended to all decisions by the Security Council on nonprocedural questions other than decisions on the peaceful settlement of disputes. Another principal weakness was the provision in the Charter narrowly limiting the authority of the U.N. to intervene in matters "essentially within the domestic jurisdiction of any state"; this provision, if given a broad interpretation, could make nonsense of many of the other provisions in the Charter.

A further cause for pessimism was the failure of the United States to display at the Conference the qualities of leadership appropriate to the greatest power in the world. The United States, as the host country, had special responsibilities for the organization of the Conference: incompetents were appointed as chairmen of committees; chairmen were given little or no guidance on procedure; as a result the committees for the first half of the Conference wasted their time on procedural wrangles. The absence of authoritative rules of procedure was almost incredible. Two weeks after the opening of the Conference the Steering Committee had still not given the chairmen of committees a ruling on the central question of voting procedure—when was a simple majority required to pass a resolution, when was a two-thirds majority required. Three weeks after the opening of the Conference the Steering Committee had not decided on the procedures for settling jurisdictional disputes between committees. On 25 May, when the Conference was at its halfway point, the rules of procedure, which had at long last been authorized by the Steering Committee, were in effect in some committees but only occasionally in others.[1]

At the very beginning of the Conference the United States put on an unwise public demonstration of its ability to deliver a majority of votes on a proposal of little or no merit which was opposed by the Soviet Union and many other countries. The Conference was supposed to be restricted to countries which had participated in the war against Germany and Japan. At Yalta, the United States, Britain, and the Soviet Union had agreed on what was meant by participation in the war. Argentina did not qualify under these criteria. Nevertheless, the United States successfully insisted that Argentina be admitted to the Conference. This demonstration that the United States had, at that time, a mechanical majority of U.N. members in its pocket, confirmed Soviet determination to protect itself against majority rule in the U.N.

Edward R. Stettinius, the head of the American delegation, and as such chairman of the fifty-nation Steering Committee and the fourteen-nation Executive Committee, was ignorant both of the substantive problems before the Conference and of how to preside at the two committees. He was so unsure of himself that at meetings he was constantly turning to his advisers with a whispered cry for help, "What do I say? What do I do now?" The two leading Democrats from Congress, Tom Connally and Sol

Bloom, chairmen of the Foreign Affairs Committees of the Senate and the House of Representatives, were no better, perhaps worse.

To the friends of the United States the American performance at San Francisco was not calculated to create confidence in the ability of the United States to provide wise leadership for the western world in the U.N. This dampened any high hopes which participants in the Conference might otherwise have had.

The roots of pessimism at the end of the San Francisco Conference went much deeper than this. The secret telegrams which we received from Ottawa about what was happening in Europe depicted a brutal Soviet occupation of half of Europe, the imposition of a puppet Soviet regime on Poland, and the breakdown of Allied cooperation in Europe. In every committee of the Conference, except the Coordination Committee, the Soviet delegates seemed intent to do all they could to ensure that the U.N. was as weak as possible. Our custom in the Canadian delegation was that the principal Canadian official on a committee would report after each committee meeting to the de facto head of the delegation, Norman Robertson. Once, when I had just begun my report, Robertson interrupted me by exclaiming, "I wish to God somebody would come into this room and not start his report by saying 'those goddamned Russians.' " In the middle of the Conference the intransigence of the Soviet Union on the veto nearly resulted in the Conference breaking up in confusion without agreement on a Charter.

Perhaps delegations which did not know much about what was happening behind the scenes at the Conference and what was happening in Europe could have high hopes at San Francisco. But the Canadian delegation was kept fully informed by Ottawa of what was happening in Europe and its close relations with the British and United States delegations meant that it knew what was happening behind the scenes at the Conference. James Reston, who covered the San Francisco Conference for the *New York Times*, and who knew more about what was happening at the Conference than all but a few of the delegates, paid a tribute twenty-four years later in his column in the *Times* to the Canadians at San Francisco:

It was the remarkable Canadian contingent at San Francisco of Mike Pearson, Norman Robertson and Escott Reid, with his own personal charter for world sanity, and all the rest of that young Canadian outfit in those critical years . . . who were closer to the divided and troubled American delegation . . . than any other delegation in the world. . . . When the chips were down the Canadians fought harder and more effectively for the principle of collective security than anybody else.[2]

14 March 1945. Wednesday.
Washington.
To father.
My ambition is to go to San Francisco for the Conference but everyone else wants to go so I am afraid there isn't much hope. I am glad Mr. King [the prime minister] has decided to appoint Conservative and C.C.F. [Cooperative Commonwealth Federation] leaders to the delegation. I wonder if, without mentioning my name, you could pass on to the "appropriate authorities," as we say in government jargon, the suggestion that special prayers be said throughout the world for the success of the San Francisco Conference during the whole time it is in session. It would have, I think, a very profound effect on the delegates. It ought to include all denominations—protestant, R.C., Orthodox—and take place in all the United Nations. Perhaps you could pass the idea on to Provost Cosgrave [of Trinity College, Toronto] and let him push it. Some large special services of intercession might take place the day the conference opens and some arrangements should be made for special services to be held if the conference should reach a crisis and be on the edge of a breakdown.

10 April 1945. Tuesday.
To mother.
My appointment as one of the technical advisers to the Canadian delegation to the San Francisco Conference has now officially come through. I leave here a week from Friday. Whether I stay for the duration of the Conference or not I do not know. Nor does anyone know how long the Conference will last. The guesses range from four to eight weeks. I am naturally delighted. It is an honour since only about four members of the Department below the rank of ambassador are being appointed as advisers. It will also be extremely interesting.

22 April 1945. Sunday.
5:00 p.m.
Kansas—Colorado border.
The trip [by special train from Washington to San Francisco] is
now almost half over and has been most enjoyable. . . . You
would have loved the Ohio valley, the first morning out. If you
had been on the train I think you would have got off, bought a
farm overlooking the river and have deserted me. . . . It was real
prairie this afternoon—completely flat to the horizon in all directions. When we stop in little towns today as we have two or three
times the whole population turns out in their Sunday best to see
us. Lord and Lady Halifax do their stuff moving graciously about
and do it very well. [Halifax was then British ambassador in
Washington.]

24 April 1945. Tuesday.
2:00 p.m.
We get into San Francisco in about two hours. Excuse the writing.
The train is jiggling badly. . . . I had a talk with Berendsen this
morning. [Carl A. Berendsen, New Zealand minister in Washington.] He and his wife were both asking after you. They like you
and wish you were here. So do I. . . . I've read on the train the
minutes of the Commonwealth meeting [on the U.N.] in London
that Hume [Wrong] went to. Berendsen says that Hume was easily
the ablest person there. Smuts didn't stand comparison with him.
[Field-Marshal J. C. Smuts, prime minister of South Africa.] A lot
of suggestions for amendment [of the Dumbarton Oaks propos-
als] were along the lines of my proposals. The British were pretty
cooperative—except on colonies—but Berendsen thinks they are
counting on the Russians to kill the proposals they don't really
like.

25 April 1945. Wednesday.
10:45 a.m.
San Francisco.
We arrived at the hotel [St. Francis] about 5:30 yesterday afternoon
[the day before the Conference opened] preceded by a motorcycle
escort—a terrifying experience, since we wound in and out of the
traffic with sirens going full blast and nearly ran down deaf old
ladies crossing on their lawful occasions with the green light. I

found after combing my hair that a delegation meeting was going
on in the P.M.'s sitting room. I went in and was effusively greeted
by the P.M. on the assumption that I was Davey Dunton. [A.
Davidson Dunton, general manager of the Wartime Information
Board.] The P.M.'s line is that the Canadian delegation is to be
helpful and not commit itself to rigid positions or, as Grant Dex-
ter puts it, it is to have no principles. When I came out of the
P.M.'s meeting Grant Dexter and Bruce Hutchison were waiting
for me to take me to dinner and to see Helen Hayes in "Harriet"—
Harriet Beecher Stowe of "Uncle Tom's Cabin." . . . [Grant
Dexter and Bruce Hutchison, newspapermen with the *Winnipeg
Free Press*.] Grant and Bruce plied me with questions about
Dumbarton Oaks until I was completely confused and then I
asked them questions about Canadian politics until I was baffled.
Grant gives the C.C.F. only 40 [seats in the forthcoming general
election], the Conservatives 70, the Liberals 100, and others 30. He
seems to expect the C.C.F. then to support the Liberals and ultimately the two parties will unite as Crerar's Progressives did with
the King tiger. I find it depressing. [In the general election which
took place on 11 June, about seven weeks later, the Liberals were
returned to power with 127 seats; the Conservatives won 67 seats,
the C.C.F. 28. Dexter had greatly underestimated Liberal strength
and overestimated the strength of the C.C.F.]

27 April 1945. Friday.
10:15 p.m.
I have been reading proofs of my [*Free World*] pamphlet late last
night and today. It is being printed here and not in New York.
. . . It ought to be out on Monday or Tuesday which will actually not be a bad time since by Tuesday or Wednesday the Conference will be getting down to business in private meetings of the
committees. Until then we shall be going through public sessions
in which each country either utters platitudes like Mr. King or
states their case like Mr. Forde, the Australian. [F. M. Forde, deputy prime minister of Australia.] . . . So far I've done virtually
no work except go to public sessions. Norman [Robertson] and
Hume [Wrong] are doing all the work themselves. They go to the
meetings of the Steering Committee with the P.M. Mike [L. B.
Pearson] feels very much left out of it and is sore. I doubt whether
he will stay here for long. Norman is being very nice to me and is

putting me on the circulation list to see all the secret telegrams which are coming in at a great rate. . . . I am a little more hopeful than I was when I came here though I have little to go on. The great powers, however, are all saying that they are willing to accept amendments. The stumbling block will be the USSR. Dana [Wilgress, ambassador in Moscow], with whom I have had a couple of meals, is depressed about the way the USSR is behaving. He feels he has misled the government by his prophecies about the moderate line which the USSR was likely to adopt after the war. (This is, of course, very secret.) The extraordinary thing about the last two days is the way in which the big three have disagreed openly in the secret sessions of the Steering Committee—mainly over Poland. It may, in the long run, turn out to be a good thing that they have disagreed and found that the world did not collapse. [E. R.] Stettinius [secretary of state of the United States] is impossible both as chairman of the Steering Committee and as chairman of the plenary sessions. He has neither dignity, suavity, intelligence or knowledge of parliamentary procedure. . . . Tonight I had dinner with Huntington Gilchrist and Van Kleffens, the Dutch minister for foreign affairs who is absurdly young looking, thin and with very narrow shoulders.

Jack Pickersgill's [J. W. Pickersgill, private secretary to the prime minister] brother, Frank, after escaping from a German internment camp a year or more ago was dropped by parachute over France in July of last year in order to serve with the Maquis. He was captured by the Germans about six weeks later and was shot in September at Buchenwald internment camp. Jack learned only a few days ago. He must have been very brave.

The big boys are trying to get the Conference concluded by May 24th. I am still betting on two months but they may succeed. It depends largely on how open to persuasion the Russians are. [My forecast of the duration of the Conference was accurate. The Conference ended on 26 June, two months and one day after it opened.]

1 May 1945. Tuesday.
3:00 p.m.
Sunday was very enjoyable. A drive into the country north of here at 11:30 a.m. to Mrs. Alexander's country house—lunch—swim—talk—Hu Shih, Etienne Dennery, Philip Jessup. [Hu Shih,

former ambassador of China in Washington. Etienne Dennery, director at the French Ministry of Foreign Affairs. Philip C. Jessup, assistant on judicial organization on the United States delegation.] Got back here about five just in time to go for a drive with Norman [Robertson] and Hume [Wrong] over the Golden Gate bridge. Did a stroke of work preparatory to a long evening of drafting amendments when Sally Reston phoned to ask me to dinner. I'd been trying to get Scotty for days. [James (Scotty) Reston of the *New York Times* and Mrs. (Sally) Reston.]

1 May 1945. Tuesday.
11:15 p.m.
We were going to spend from 4:15 on working on amendments—Norman, Hume, [L.] Rasminsky [assistant to the governor of the Bank of Canada] and myself. First we spent an hour on committee assignments. Then the delegates met for an hour with the P.M. Afterwards it took us 2½ hours to have a dinner downstairs of soup, liver and coffee. So we have adjourned till tomorrow morning. The Conference has gone through many crises. Stettinius is an utter incompetent and the sooner it is found essential that he return to important work in Washington the better. . . . He does not know the first thing about parliamentary procedure or how to run a committee. He was responsible for the Russians being virtually isolated on a procedural question relating to the admission of Argentina (they asked for postponement of the decision). [On 13 May, twelve days after I wrote this letter, Senator Arthur H. Vandenberg, ranking Republican member of the Senate Foreign Relations Committee, wrote in his diary, "Stettinius does not have a seasoned grasp of foreign affairs. He rarely contributes to our policy discussions (at meetings of the United States delegation)"[3]] There may be something to be said for slapping the Russians down in public but Stettinius chose an issue where they can most easily make it appear that right and justice are on their side. The Russians won a complete victory on everything except the vote and are feeling very happy. That doesn't matter. What does matter is that we have given them good grounds for saying that even on a procedural question the dice are loaded against them by the western powers and that they therefore must be sure to keep a veto over as many decisions of the Council as possible. You can tell Mark [Marquis Childs, American columnist] all the above but

don't tell him Molotov's [V. M. Molotov, people's commissar for foreign affairs of the Soviet Union] remark in committee today when he pointed out that a decision to let the Conference decide by majority vote meant that the vote of 20 [Latin] American Republics, plus the Philippines and Liberia (which were all in the pocket of one state) needed only 1½ votes to constitute a majority. It is very depressing that on almost the very day of victory in Europe we should be fighting with the Russians on questions all over Europe and on trivial questions here such as chairmanships and Argentina. It doesn't hold out much promise for the future. It now looks as if the Conference will not really get down to business until next Monday when we will be going into committees. Some of the committees are going to be chaotic since the chairmanships have been distributed purely on a prestige basis among the various states and, even with good luck, half the chairmen are likely to be incompetent. We would never expect to win a war if we distributed generalships on this basis. Why we should hope to win a peace by doing this I don't know. In this atmosphere the news from Europe seems remote. The war is ending not with a bang but a whimper. The dictators are being bumped off. Germany is—in the Berlin area at least—being reduced into chaos. Perhaps when most of the politicians leave in about a week's time the rest of us will be able to pull some half-decent charter out of this mess but I am doubtful whether we are going to succeed in improving Dumbarton Oaks as much as I had hoped when I came here. There's nothing I can do except sit and smoulder and hope my pamphlet will do some good when it appears. If it isn't out tomorrow I shall shoot someone.

4 May 1945. Friday.
11:00 p.m.
Last night I had Sally and Scotty Reston to dinner to meet Dana [Wilgress]. They phoned at the last moment to bring Lois and Eric Sevareid (CBS commentator). You would like them both. . . . We had one of the best meals of my life at an Armenian restaurant called "Omar Khayam's." Before the dinner we had a delegation meeting—the first for about a week. The P.M. was extraordinarily irresponsible and stupid. The purpose of the meeting was to discuss amendments. He disclaimed all responsibility for the ones we had drafted and then objected to defining an

object of the Economic and Social Council as raising standards of living *for all*. He thought we should aim at raising standards only in poor countries because otherwise they would compete against us unfairly. I had hoped that some delegations might be persuaded to father some of my amendments [in my pamphlet] but they got them too late to make this possible. However they may exert an influence in the discussions in spite of that. Anyway my conscience is pretty clear because I did what I could. If the bombs start falling again that may make me feel a little happier. We are now in the doldrums. All the public speeches are over. All amendments have to be in by tonight. Until the amendments are all in and organized the committees can't get down to business. So yesterday, today and tomorrow we are just playing about getting the committees organized. On Monday we get down to business.

About a week ago when I saw Scotty [Reston] the subject came up of the autograph hunters in the lobby of the St. Francis. I invented the story that whenever, working in my little room, I got depressed at my futility and anonymity I would go to the lobby and sign autographs for ten minutes and then come back to work greatly refreshed. The story is moving around with great rapidity and bumped back at me today. I may become famous for that story but not for my constitution [my *Free World* proposals for a U.N. Charter].

4 May 1945. Friday.
To father.
It is too soon to say what is going to come out of this conference. Things were badly handled during the first week—silly fights over chairmanships and Argentina, on the latter of which the Russians put the western powers badly in the wrong. The problem of keeping peace over the next thirty years is that of keeping peace between the Soviet Union on the one hand and the U.S. and the U.K. on the other. It is silly to lose sight of that objective. . . . This is a lovely city—one of the loveliest in the world. The weather has been almost perfect.

6 May 1945. Sunday.
1:45 p.m.
To son, Patrick.
The conference looks a little brighter now than it did last week.

The big four have agreed on some improvements in the proposals. But the general outlook for the future is not too encouraging. It is going to be a long, hard and dreary fight for the next fifty years to keep the nations of the world from having another big war again.

7 May 1945. Monday.
6:10 p.m.
I had a committee meeting this morning where I was Gordon Graydon's adviser. [Graydon, leader of the Conservative opposition in the House of Commons.] We sat back and said nothing and let the New Zealanders do the work. In general New Zealand and Australia are doing the things which we would do if we had any guts. We would also, I think, do them better. This afternoon I did a short speech for Graydon to give tomorrow. It is completely innocuous and is a plea for clear language. There is one good paragraph at the end but that will probably be struck out.

It is unbelievable that today is the end of the war in Europe. There is no sign of excitement on the streets but everyone is going about their business as usual. When the news gradually seeps into our minds we shall feel happier. No matter how terrible the conditions are in the world today and no matter how grim our fears are of the future one need not any longer be tortured by the thought of armies of men killing each other in Europe, of cities being destroyed, of millions of people being callously mistreated and slaughtered in Germany and occupied Europe. Terrible things are going to happen in Europe but they will not be as terrible as what has happened. (Be very sure that the children don't go to a movie at which they are showing the atrocity films of the German concentration camps.)

Grant Dexter took me to dinner last night and when we came back at about ten we went to see Norman and Hume and stayed till midnight talking (they not I) about King and Canadian politics. The more you learn of the little man the more despicable he is. If the Liberals go into opposition Grant thinks they may pick Doug Abbott of Montreal as leader. [Douglas C. Abbott, minister of national defence for naval services.] Everyone seems to agree that whether he wins or not King has only two more years to go. He has aged a lot. I told Grant of my feeling that I ought to get out of the [External Affairs] service soon. He was shocked but he didn't say much to convince me I shouldn't except that I was one of the three or four top people in the department at which I snorted. As a horrible example he told me that Johnny Deutsch isn't happy as an editorial writer because he finds it impossible to write to to-morrow morning's deadline. [John Deutsch had recently resigned from the Department of External Affairs to join the *Winnipeg Free Press*.]

There is nothing interesting about the Conference I can think of to tell you. I am not certain I have told you before that the amendments moved by the four sponsoring powers are better than I feared. They have gone some way to meet criticisms. It may, however, represent pretty well their last word but my guess is that they may recede a little on a number of minor points but hold firm on the rest. I said to Grant the other day that it was "Half a League, Half a League, Half a League Onward." Grant capped by continuing with the next line. "Into the valley of death rode the six hundred." Fortunately, however, the actual delegates number closer to 300 than to 600.

8 May 1945. Tuesday.
9:30 p.m.
Last night I went to the free movie to see the new Gershwin film and on our way back to the hotel (I was with Gordon Robertson) we met John Carter Vincent. [Gordon Robertson, Department of External Affairs. Vincent, chief, division of Chinese affairs, State Department.] The streets were quieter last night than even on or-dinary nights. No sign of celebration of the end of the war [in Europe]. I felt we could not let armistice night pass without some celebration so asked Vincent up for a drink. Vincent didn't stay late but Jack Pickersgill did. Today has been a holiday in S.F. but even that has not resulted in any sign of relief or excitement. The Pacific war is too close to S.F. for them to be particularly inter-ested in the end of the war in Europe.

The committees are still going on doing virtually nothing. Each one of the twelve committees gets involved in a long, tedious and futile debate on how to go about discussing the questions they are going to discuss. The debates don't lead anywhere because the decisions on procedural questions have to be made by the steering committee. If only the steering committee had made them a week ago we might have been able to get down to business before now. St. Laurent [Louis St. Laurent, minister of justice] had to leave

the committee I was in this morning, and I was left in sole possession on behalf of Canada. I put the fear of God in Norman by
telling him I had voted on behalf of Canada. He said that he
hoped I was on the same side as a sizeable number of other delegates. He was greatly relieved when I told him that the motion had
been passed unanimously. The motion was that the committee
stop discussing procedural questions and go on to discussing a
question of substance—what should be the conditions of membership in the new organization.

Tomorrow evening I have asked John Carter Vincent to have
dinner with Wilgress and myself. We'll learn all about China.

10 May 1945. Thursday.
12:25 p.m.
They are now starting to hold committees four times a day—
10:30, 2:45, 5:00 and 8:30. Yesterday I had committees for the three
last periods. The committees remind me of the Englishman's explanation of why British films were almost always a flop in
England—"The Englishman will die for his country but he will
not be bored for it." We would not be bored if we weren't gagged
and unable to say anything but that is pretty much our position.
At the meeting of our delegation this morning I had to raise the
question whether we should vote for the Australian proposal to
limit the veto of individual great powers over the admission of
new members solely to ex-enemy states. By the end of the discussion almost everyone was on the verge of losing his temper. The
discussion became a controversy between the advisers plus Coldwell [M. J. Coldwell, parliamentary leader of the Cooperative
Commonwealth Federation], and St. Laurent and Graydon plus
Pearson. I now realize better Mike's ability to rise in favour. He is
agile at quitting a position when he finds that the powers don't
like it. [This criticism was unfair. Pearson's normal strategy was
to retire from an exposed position in order to make possible a
successful attack later.] Rasminsky went far out on a limb, [War-
wick] Chipman [ambassador to Chile] some distance and I think I
did little more than present a reasoned argument for supporting
the Australian amendment even if it were opposed by all the great
powers. Coldwell and Mrs. Casselman [Mrs. Cora T. Casselman,
Conservative member of parliament] are gradually waking up to
the futility of our presence here and to the weakness of the new

organization. I now find myself trying to persuade them that, in spite of its imperfections, it can be made to serve a useful purpose. [Canada voted for the Australian proposal but it was defeated.]

12 May 1945. Friday.
4:00 p.m.
I have just given Miss Mather two speeches to type, one for Graydon and one for Mrs. Casselman so I now have some spare time. I had three committees on Wednesday, two on Thursday and two today, one this morning and one this evening. . . . The Conference drags ahead against obstacles of incredible magnitude. The committees appear to be seized by a morbid fear of discussing the substance of questions and consequently spend their time discussing procedure. A committee is doing well if it spends no more than its first hour discussing procedure. The worst yet was one which met from 5:00 to 7:30 yesterday evening on structures and procedures of the Assembly where I was advising Coldwell. We were discussing the simple question whether each great power should have the right to veto the admission of new members. After a long wrangle on procedure—whether or not to start by discussing the Australian amendment—we reached at six o'clock a long speech by Sol Bloom [Democrat chairman of the Foreign Affairs Committee of the House of Representatives] in which he (a) read Webster's definition of security; (b) said he had received letters written in blood; (c) said he had had to be accompanied to his office by two secret policemen; (d) appealed to us not to betray those who had suffered in the war. All this had nothing to do with the subject before the committee. By seven o'clock the committee was in a state of hysterics due to the unutterable confusion. Nobody knew what resolution was before the committee. The chairman who had previously been permitting complete anarchy decided as a weak man will that he should become a dictator. He insisted we vote on all seven amendments submitted to the article. Half the time the amendments were not read or, if read, translated. They were all rejected and so he then said he would put the Dumbarton Oaks draft which was carried in a partly deserted meeting by a bare two-thirds. We voted in favour of the Australian amendment and then abstained on all the rest as a sign of our contempt at the disorder.

Afterwards Coldwell and I had a stiff drink of whisky and had a pleasant dinner together. I was asleep by 11:30 and slept till 8:00 with no pill or even bromide.

Another chairman suddenly started having translations made into Russian as well as into French and English though this was contrary to the regulations. He was just being very courteous. Latins love talking about procedure. Many chairmen are Latins and no Latin chairman will ever call another Latin to order or choke off debate for fear of interfering with the solidarity of Latin America. This morning's meeting demonstrated conclusively the virtual impossibility of parliamentary democracy working in Latin America. The Latin way of conducting a meeting is to let everyone propose resolutions and talk on them as long as he likes, allow anyone to go back to something already decided and to exert no control. In addition to this accidental confusion we may be faced with a conspiracy on the part of some of the big three to encourage the snarling up of discussions so that in an atmosphere of frustration the Conference will decide to agree to the Dumbarton Oaks proposals because they can't reach agreement on anything else. On top of all this I am sure the French have organized the use of French so that people speak French who could probably speak English better and the Russians, even though they can speak French or English, insist on speaking Russian. A Russian secretary from their embassy in London had to translate for [A. A.] Gromyko [ambassador in Washington] this morning. I pitied him because Gromyko who understands English very well kept correcting him. . . . Parts of my pamphlet have appeared in *Free World*. I haven't got copies yet but when I do I'll send you one. I am afraid it will have virtually no results here.

13 May 1945. Sunday.
11:30 p.m.
To mother.
The Conference is full of dullness and discussion that only slowly gets anywhere. Making peace is like making war. It is ten parts boredom and one part excitement. The chairmen of committees are utterly incompetent. They will never stop anyone from talking no matter how irrelevant his remarks may be. And the Latins love arguing for hours over points of procedure so instead of spending time getting anywhere we spend our time discussing how to get somewhere. But the city is really lovely. It is the kind of

city one can fall in love with at first sight. . . . The job which we are going to do here will not be first rate but the document will I hope be better than the thing we started with.

13 May 1945. Sunday.
11:45 p.m.
Gordon Robertson and I got ourselves driven today to the other side of the Golden Gate Bridge—about two miles beyond—and then walked back. It was the kind of day when fog and drizzle intermitted with bright sun. The bridge is really one of the great wonders of man. It has to be walked over to be appreciated. The great sweeps of the suspension cables, the towers like great Norman towers, the long views on both sides. Walking up from the town on the other side, Sausolito, was like walking in the south of France. The same rich smell of flowers, and hills coming down to the water. . . .

The only cheerful thing to report is that the chairmen are being brought under some control by the secretariat so that the committee meetings are a little less anarchic. I discovered a truth the other day which was received by Jim Green with some approbation. [James F. Green, special assistant to the secretary-general of the Conference.] I said that the advantage of diplomats over politicians at a conference like this was that they gave shorter speeches, the reason being that a diplomat disliked so much what he had to say that he said it in as few words as possible. . . . Take care of yourself and keep on missing me though why you should I don't know because I haven't been much of a source of cheerfulness and affection around the house for a long time. Perhaps now that I don't have to be haunted by the thought of millions of men fighting in Europe I can become more at peace with myself.

At San Francisco and in London the Soviet Union made a determined effort to ensure that the Secretariat of the U.N. would have neither competence nor independence. On one occasion at San Francisco the Soviet Union succeeded in persuading the United States, Britain, and China to join it in proposing an amendment to the Dumbarton Oaks proposals on the Secretariat which would have weakened the Secretariat. The Dumbarton Oaks proposals had stipulated that the secretary-general should be the chief administrative officer and should be elected by the

General Assembly on the recommendation of the Security Council. This meant that each of the great powers would have a veto on the appointment. The amendment proposed at San Francisco by the four powers was that there should be four deputy secretaries-general appointed in the same way as the secretary-general, so that the great power veto would extend to all five senior officers of the Secretariat.

I was representing Canada on the committee on the Secretariat and had been given instructions to oppose the proposal. The chairman of the committee insisted that he would put the proposal to a vote without any debate on it. Perhaps he was being stupid, like so many of the committee chairmen at San Francisco. Perhaps he had been instructed by one or more of the great powers to ram the proposal through without debate. I protested his ruling and after many rebuffs managed to secure permission to give a speech. This started off a heated debate which went on for many weeks and the proposal was eventually defeated.

The four great powers were not agreed on the intent of their proposal. The intent of the Soviet delegation was that the secretary-general and the four deputies would rotate among the five permanent members of the Security Council; the terms of appointment would be for two years so that within ten years each of the five would have a national as secretary-general. Anthony Eden and Stettinius, on the other hand, were opposed to restricting appointments to the five powers.[4] Nevertheless, two weeks after they had stated their opposition the Soviet delegation was still hoping that their proposal for rotation would succeed.[5] By 26 May it looked to the United States delegation that the four powers could not get their proposal through the committee.[6] By 17 June, when the issue came to a vote in the committee, the great powers were proposing five deputy secretaries-general instead of four. Gromyko had stated at a five-power meeting that this would make it possible to have one deputy secretary-general from outside the group of five.[7] Forty-five countries would have one deputy secretary-general. Five countries would have four deputies and the secretary-general.

In the voting in committee the proposal for four or five deputy secretaries-general received a simple majority of the votes cast, but not the necessary two-thirds majority, and the original Dumbarton Oaks proposal making no mention of deputy secretaries-general was adopted. The great powers capitulated; they agreed not to press for a reconsideration of the vote.[8]

15 May 1945.
9:30 p.m.
My guess is that the conference is about half over—that is that it will end about June 8. But it may spin out until June 25. . . . I gave an American the other day my motto for the Conference— "Per ardua ad cartam castratam" [which I hoped was Latin for "through difficulties to a castrated charter"] and he replied with the motto of a member of the American delegation taken from Stettinius' constant remarks at meetings to his advisers—"What'll I do? What'll I say?"

Yesterday evening I made my first speech at the conference. I was left alone at the evening meeting on the Assembly when the four power proposal for the appointment of four deputy secretaries-general on nomination by the [Security] Council came up. I was instructed to oppose it but in order to get the floor I had to go through half an hour of devious parliamentary wrangling because the chairman wanted to take a vote without discussion. Fortunately Rasminsky came in just as this item was coming up and advised me on tactics. He was supposed to do the speaking but since I had to raise the points of order as he hadn't been at the previous meeting Lou felt I ought to carry on. In order to get the floor I had to pretend I had a speech to deliver and then, when my bluff was called, had to invent one. It went off all right and may have resulted in killing the proposal. The vote on it takes place tomorrow morning.

I got Clyde Eagleton to introduce me to Stassen today. [Eagleton, division of international organization affairs, State Department. Commander Harold E. Stassen, Republican.] I said I had debated against him at Hart House [University of Toronto] in 1926. He recalled the subject of the debate—"That the influence of the U.S. on Canada has increased, is increasing, and ought to be diminished," the remarks made by one Canadian about Elks and Moose and the reply. No wonder he is a good politician. I don't know whether I mentioned in previous letters the impression Stassen has made on the Conference. He and Vandenberg are definitely the strong men on the U.S. delegation and he is extremely charming, courteous and intelligent. His chances of getting the

Republican nomination [for the presidency] have gone up tre-
mendously during the past two weeks. One of the few good results
of this Conference is the influence of Vandenberg and Stassen on
the foreign delegates. Most foreigners believe that all the interna-
tionalists are in the Democratic ranks. They find here that the
Democrats are incompetent bumbling ranters—Stettinius who
ought to be head of the National Y.M.C.A. of the U.S., Connally
and Bloom who are overbearing and stupid. From now on a Republican victory—if Stassen and Vandenberg are Republican
leaders—will not mean that terrible sinking feeling abroad which
it might otherwise have meant. [Pearson, a month before the Conference opened, forecast in a despatch to Ottawa that it seemed
likely that Vandenberg and Stassen might well be the most influential members of the United States delegation at San Francisco. "They outrank in ability and in popular appeal Senator
Connally, Congressman Bloom and Congressman Eaton."]

The main fight from now on will be over the veto especially
as applied to the peaceful settlement of disputes and to the
amendment procedure; over the bloody four-power reservation on
domestic jurisdiction which makes nonsense of a great part of the
charter; over trusteeship. I am afraid the chances of getting a declaration of the rights of man have gone by the board. The western
powers are playing into the hands of the Russians. Russian influence as well as armies are pushing forward into Europe to fill a
vacuum and the western powers are doing nothing themselves to
fill the vacuum by providing a dynamic creed. Instead it looks
from Churchill's speech that all they are doing is creating an alliance against the Soviet Union.

16 May 1945.
Memorandum for Mr. Pearson, with copies to N. A. Robertson
and L. Rasminsky.
Appointment of the personnel of the secretariat.
. . . The original Dumbarton Oaks proposals did not contain
any provision providing for the appointment of Deputy
Secretaries-General. One of the four-great-power amendments,
however, is to paragraph 1 of Chapter X, and this reads as follows
[the passages italicized being the amendment]:

> There should be a Secretariat comprising a Secretary-
> General, *four deputies* and such staff as may be required. *The*

Secretary-General and his deputies should be elected by the General Assembly on recommendation of the Security Council for a period of three years, and the Secretary-General should be eligible for reelection. The Secretary-General should be the chief administrative officer of the Organization. . . .

The four-power proposal is . . . open to the objection that it provides for the election of the five senior officers of the Organization on the same basis. The consequence would be that a Deputy Secretary-General would be in a position to be able to say to the Secretary-General that he was not responsible to him, but that his responsibility, like that of the Secretary-General, was to the body which had elected him. This would be inconsistent with the principle laid down in the Dumbarton Oaks proposals that the Secretary-General shall be "the chief administrative officer of the Organization." It might indeed lead to the government of the international civil service by a five-member committee, and it would be wholly undesirable that every important administrative decision involving the Secretariat should have to be made by a committee of five. No one can now say, before the Organization is even set up, that four Deputy Secretaries-General will be required. It is therefore inadvisable to mention any specific number in the Charter. It is indeed difficult not to interpret the fact that the great four have proposed five senior officers to mean that they intend that each of them should designate one of the senior officers. . . . The other main argument against political appointees in the higher posts is that it will inevitably result in the international civil servants of the nationality of the higher officer feeling that they owe their allegiance to him and taking their directions from him and not from the Secretary-General.

18 May 1945. Friday.
11:45 p.m.
The conference still makes progress very slowly. My guess is that the big questions will all be decided next week and then the heat will be turned on to complete the odds and ends. This would put the end of the conference about three weeks from today. All the evening meetings and the general feeling of frustration of the delegations from the smaller countries are beginning to lead to loss of tempers. I was at a rather nasty meeting on Wednesday

night of the committee on political and security functions of the
Assembly. I had notes written out, on instructions from Norman
to give a "gracious" speech welcoming the initiative of the great
five in proposing new amendments strengthening the powers of
the Assembly. Fortunately I didn't give it at the opening of the
session because no sooner had it got under way than the Soviet
moved an amendment (which was really a joker) to the big-five
amendment and the U.K. supported them. They forced it through
18 to 3 with about 18 abstentions including myself. This left a bad
taste in everybody's mouth and from then on things went from
bad to worse with scarcely veiled threats from Latins, Arabs and
New Zealanders that if they were going to be disregarded in this
way they weren't going to sign the Charter. . . .

The important things are not happening here but elsewhere.
It looks very much as if the world is beginning to jell into two
rival groups—the Soviet and the Anglo-American. The new
League being established here can work only if there is an extremely high degree of cooperation between the three great powers. The chances of our getting that cooperation seem pretty slim
from what is going on today throughout the world. Perhaps we
are not going through the blackest period but it certainly is pretty
black. It's time I got to bed before I get even more dismal and
follow my usual way adown Titanic glooms of chasmed fears.

21 May 1945. Monday.
9:40 p.m.
The weekend was very successful. We [Dana Wilgress, Major-
General Maurice Pope, military secretary to the Cabinet War
Committee, and I] left at three on Saturday afternoon, arrived at
Carmel about seven, left at five on Sunday and got back about
ten-thirty after dinner en route. I came back very burned by the
sun and wind. I thought we were going to stay at some simple
place in Carmel but discovered when we got there that it was of the
style though not the size of Hot Springs and all I had with me was
what I was wearing, my old brown jacket and my new flannels.
The hotel had been much impressed by the major-generalship of
Pope and the ambassadorship of Wilgress. We were met by the
hostess who invited us to have cocktails with her. After cocktails
she shepherded us to dinner and ordered wine for us. Salvador
Dali and his wife were at the cocktail party of about a dozen. He

looks like a complete show-off—small black moustache, and black hair curling around his collar. During the party there took place the mystery of the exploding tumbler. We were having old-fashioneds. One man finished his, put it on a table with ice still in it. Shortly afterward it exploded into a dozen bits with a big bang. The orthodox explanation is that a German scientist exploded it from 10,000 miles away.

The drive along the coast from Monterey to Carmel—about 17 miles—is lovely—wild rocks coming down to a blue sea. We drove in the morning stopping off every now and then for a walk along the coast. We stayed for a long time watching the seals, playing about in the water and on the rocks. I've decided that if I'm reincarnated I should like to be a seal on the rocks off Carmel. They seem perfectly happy. They do nothing but play, swim, bark, eat and breed. They never seem to lose their tempers or do anybody any harm except to the fish they eat. I think they are true Christians.

The international situation seems to be getting worse again. It's like in the old days before the war. Norman [Robertson] uses extreme language for him—"thoroughly disturbing and alarming." It's pretty discouraging.

Perhaps you have heard of the death almost on the last day of the war of Mr. Symington's only son—twenty-nine years old. I am very unhappy at the thought of how it will affect him. I must write him today or tomorrow. [H. J. Symington had been head of the Canadian delegation to the conference on international civil aviation in Chicago in 1944.]

There were two committees which gave cause for hope for the future of the United Nations. One was the Coordination Committee at San Francisco; the other, the Executive Committee of the Preparatory Commission of the United Nations, in London. Paul Hasluck of Australia, who like me served on both committees, and who afterwards was Australian representative on the Security Council during its early months, has written that these two committees "met more obscurely and more quietly" than the Security Council but their "achievement was much more encouraging than that of the Security Council."[9] Both committees were composed of the same fourteen countries: the five permanent members of the Security Council (China, France, the Soviet Union, the

United Kingdom, and the United States) and nine others elected
by the San Francisco Conference (Australia, Brazil, Canada,
Chile, Czechoslovakia, Iran, Mexico, Netherlands, and Yugoslavia).

As soon as any of the twelve so-called technical committees of
the San Francisco Conference approved of a paragraph of the
Charter it was sent to the Coordination Committee, whose duty it
was to revise it if it did not clearly express the intent of the technical committee. The Coordination Committee was also required to
review all the paragraphs to make sure that they were consistent
with each other in terminology, form and substance and to arrange them in logical sequence by articles and chapters. The
Coordination Committee, as Paul Hasluck has put it, had direct
links with the Dumbarton Oaks Conference where the three great
powers had drawn up the first plan for a world organization. Its
chairman, Dr. Leo Pasvolsky of the United States delegation; the
Soviet representatives, A. A. Sobolev and S. A. Golunsky; the
United Kingdom representatives, Gladwyn Jebb and C. K. Webster, had all helped to draft the Dumbarton Oaks proposals,
which were the basis of discussion at San Francisco. "It was only
necessary for someone to question the use of a comma in such and
such a line of such and such a paragraph for them to produce
immediately the high reasons of state that had led to the insertion
of the comma in the first place."[10]

The Coordination Committee owed much of its success to
Leo Pasvolsky, who was the State Department's principal expert
on the Charter. He realized that in this kind of committee it was
essential not to take votes but to weigh opinions. If discussion
showed that a proposal was opposed by a great power he would
say, "Since there is not general agreement I suggest we let this
matter stand over till our next meeting," hoping that by then the
great power would have withdrawn its opposition or that a compromise would have been worked out. If a smaller power were in a
minority he would say, "I assume that in the light of the general
agreement on this point the delegate of———will not wish to
press his objection."

There was one time when this ploy did not work. We were
discussing the preamble. There was general agreement that "we
the peoples of the United Nations" would not only be "determined" to do certain things but would also agree to the Charter of

the U.N. The Netherlands delegate, Adrian Pelt, objected. Under Netherlands law it was only the monarch who could agree to a treaty. The Netherlands government could not sign a Charter which said that the people of the Netherlands agreed to a treaty. At first most of the members of the Coordination Committee were not inclined to take this nice constitutional point seriously. But Pelt persisted and the committee was forced to find a formula which would satisfy him. The peoples of the United Nations would be determined to do certain things but it was their governments which would agree to the Charter.

At the Dumbarton Oaks Conference, when the great powers could not reach complete agreement on a provision to be included in the Charter, they would mask their disagreement in deliberately obscure language. One example is Article 107:

> Nothing in the present Charter shall invalidate or preclude action, in relation to any state which during the Second World War has been an enemy of any signatory to the present Charter, taken or authorized as a result of that war by the Governments having responsibility for such action.

Norman Robertson suggested at a meeting of the Coordination Committee that something should be done to elucidate the meaning of this article. Pasvolsky said, "Norman, if I were you I would let sleeping dogs lie particularly when they are such very large dogs."

The Coordination Committee made a considerable number of changes in the draft statute of the International Court of Justice in order that the terminology of the statute should conform to the terminology of the Charter of which it forms an integral part. It failed, because of the opposition of the leading jurists at the Conference, to make other improvements in the statute. The jurists, for instance, insisted on no amendments to the barbarous first section of Article 40 with its "cases," "case," and "case." "Cases are brought before the Court, as the case may be, either by the notification of the special agreement or by a written application addressed to the Registrar. In either case the subject of the dispute and the parties shall be indicated."

A panel of language experts met next door to the Coordination Committee. Their task was to translate the English text agreed to by the Coordination Committee into equally authentic

French, Russian, Spanish, and Chinese texts. The only one of these translations which the Coordination Committee kept a careful eye on was the French but on one occasion it got involved in the Russian text. We were discussing Chapter II of the Charter on membership. The question under discussion was whether we should refer to the member states of the U.N. as member states or simply as members. There was general agreement that we would call them "Members." The Soviet representative said that he could go along with this decision, provided it was understood that in the Russian text, the term "Member States" would be used and not "Members," since the word, *member*, meant in Russian the male sex organ.

The Soviet representatives on the committee were, to begin with, suspicious that, under the guise of making drafting improvements, the western members would make changes of substance calculated to weaken the Soviet position in the U.N. After only a few meetings of the committee they realized that the western members had no such intention; all they wanted was to produce as workmanlike a job as possible; to remove inconsistencies, unintentional obscurities, and clumsy structure and language from the draft articles of the Charter which had been approved by the committees of the Conference. From then on the Soviet representatives were among the most ardent and intelligent craftsmen on the committee. Golunsky, and not the French representative, soon became the acknowledged expert on ensuring that the French text was as good or better than the English text. My experience as the adviser to the Canadian member of the committee gave me hope that in the U.N. it might be possible to have first-rate committees of experts.

23 May 1945. Wednesday.
4:45 p.m.
Today is the first weekday for a very long time when I have had no meetings in the afternoon and evening. I have spent the afternoon clearing up papers. I intended to go for a long walk but Scotty Reston phoned to see me and spent a half hour with me getting assistance for his story in tomorrow's *Times*. He is looking utterly exhausted but is doing work which merits him a second Pulitzer prize.

Norman has given me a job I like. Hume and I are his advisers on the Coordination Committee which consists of one representative of each of the 14 nations on the Executive Committee. [Hume Wrong, being busy on other matters, did not act as adviser to Robertson on the Coordination Committee so I became the sole adviser.] The Coordination Committee goes over the texts of the Charter prepared by the Technical Committees so this will give me a chance to try at least to get the Charter written in something approaching English. So far I have been at two meetings of the C.C. It had previously been spending its time telling the other committees not to waste time. But its activities reminded me of the parable to the mote and the beam. It spent its time discussing for hours the proper arrangement and order of the articles in the Charter—whether purposes came before principles or *vice versa*, whether organs came before membership or *vice versa*, whether there should be Parts, Chapters and Articles, or no Parts or no Chapters. The only cheerful thing was that when we finally did get down to discussing the actual text of an article, the committee decided it was so badly written that it would have to be completely rewritten.

Last night I had to go to a meeting of "Dominion" representatives with the British who tried to persuade us to withdraw our opposition (Canada, Australia, N.Z.) to the great-power proposal that they should nominate four deputy secretaries-general as well as the Secretary-General. I was polite so long as Gladwyn Jebb was running the meeting but began to be a little pointed when C. K. Webster intervened. He is a domineering professor who speaks like God Almighty to Job. Afterwards Lou [Rasminsky] and I argued with Norman for an hour to try to persuade him not to force us to withdraw our opposition. The argument continued at the delegation meeting this morning with a partial victory for us. The anti-climax was that the issue never came up since the committee got all tangled up in the question of the Secretary-General and never got to the deputies.

24 May 1945. Thursday.
To father.

I think the final Charter is going to be better than the Dumbarton Oaks proposals but not as good as what was politically possible. The main obstacle is, of course, the suspicion between the western world and the Soviet Union. We have to tailor a char-

ter not for Wilkie's "One World" but for a globe which consists of
two worlds. Our hope has to be that in the course of the next few
decades the two worlds can learn to understand each other and to
progress first to the point at which each does not believe the other
is out to dominate it and then to the point at which a lack of
mistrust becomes a positive trust.

There is nothing today to fear but fear. The Soviet Union is
not, I am sure, planning how to secure world domination by force
but they sometimes act in such a way as to frighten the western
world. The western world is not planning to overthrow the Soviet
Union by force but apparently we unknowingly do things which
lead the Soviet Union to suspect that we do. Thus we both get
frightened and fear is a bad counsellor. From false fears good Lord
deliver us.

We all have a feeling here that what we are doing is merely
writing marginal notes on the pages of history. The substance of
history is being written not in San Francisco but in Poland, Germany, Czechoslovakia, Yugoslavia and so on. That is where the
new world is taking shape, and taking shape with terrifying
speed. I told Norman Robertson the other day that probably the
root of our troubles was the failure of the Council of Nicaea (or
was it another Council) to find a formula which would have prevented the schism between the Eastern and Western churches. The
political schism in Europe today runs along much the same geo-
graphic lines as the ancient schism between the Orthodox and the
Catholic churches.

25 May 1945. Friday.
4:20 p.m.
Scotty Reston did a brilliant job in his article in this morning's
New York Times summarizing the results of one month's work by
the Conference. I enclose a copy as it appeared in the special edition of the *New York Times* which is published for members of
the Conference. The children might like to show this facsimile
edition at their school, but please keep Scotty's article. . . . I
wrote Dad a long letter last night and have sent Mother a copy of
today's *New York Times*. Without being dishonest I tried to be as
cheerful as I could in my letter to Dad. In general I took much the
same line as Scotty. . . .

Something big has to be done soon to stop the steadily increasing speed with which we are setting about to construct two

rival, heavily armed camps in the world. I wish I felt that Churchill and Truman are big men but I can't, and the longer the big constructive move is put off the more difficult the problems become.

27 May 1945. Sunday.
7:00 p.m.
Friday evening was a nervous occasion for me. Chipman had to take the chair in the committee on the political and security functions of the Assembly and I therefore had to be acting delegate. Norman came in but wouldn't take my place. An amendment was up giving the Assembly power to submit the Security Council to a sort of third-degree. We were opposing it as unnecessary and as an unwise indication of mistrust of the Council. The debate got very heated. The Belgians talked about the Assembly being, if not a collection of mutes, at least a collection of stutterers. Norman thought I should speak and I therefore had to speak extempore just before Vandenberg. I was nervous beforehand but it was not so bad once I had begun speaking especially since the Dutch member of the Committee for whom I have great respect gave me encouraging glances as I went along. When Vandenberg got up he said in his rotund style that the distinguished delegate from Canada had given the speech which he intended to give. Afterwards Norman said that the level of debate had been very high and that the two best speeches were by Vandenberg and myself. He also asked me if I felt like the Austrian soldier at Solferino who had been wounded fighting on the wrong side, adding that in any event I had given no indication of not believing what I was saying. Actually I did believe in what I had to say. The episode ought to help to overcome the story which seems to have been sedulously spread in Ottawa that I cannot be depended on to be moderate in my language at conference meetings. . . .

When I was still sleeping at 9:15 this morning Barney Nover phoned. [Barnet Nover of the *Washington Post.*] He had been here for a couple of days and had been trying to get in touch with me. I asked him to have breakfast with me in half an hour and he stayed till 12:15. The two phrases of mine which I think he will use are that we ought to be more concerned with the powerlessness of the Security Council than with its power and that the Assembly is a second line of defence against war—the Council being the first line. . . .

The only amusing thing which happened yesterday was in the discussion of the report of the rapporteur of the committee on structure and procedures of the Assembly. The report was, of course, written by the secretary, an American civil servant. The rapporteur is a Byelorussian who had said not a word at any meeting of the committee. The report had been circulated the day before in English and in French. The rapporteur, however, read it in Russian and every time he finished a paragraph the English and French versions were then read by translators. I got the *N.Y. Times* out under the table and read all its four pages. In the report it was explained that one reason the committee had decided in favour of each country having five representatives in the Assembly was that "member states, especially those with many shades of political opinion, could secure the advantages of consultation within their delegation." I grinned as soon as I read it. The Soviet representative as soon as it was read aloud requested that the paragraph be amended either by striking out the reason or by giving a variety of reasons. Though no one said anything the committee saw the humour of it. . . .

My latest motto for the Conference is—"An expense of spirit in a waste of shame."

31 May 1945. Thursday.
5:00 p.m.
I am now spending most of my time working with Norman on the Coordination Committee. At present it isn't as intensive as other work but it involves a good deal of time hanging around waiting to get a chance to go over the documents with Norman. What would take 45 minutes of uninterrupted time takes two hours of interrupted time. The work however is interesting and it gives me a chance to improve the language and structure of the Charter and occasionally a chance of influencing a decision on a point of substance. But it is going to be a pretty hypocritical document as well as wordy.

Last night I went to a very nice party at a Mrs. Rogers who was at high school with Norman in Vancouver. She was very charming and her three children were almost the same age as ours. Lilah Rasminsky, who is now here, called my bluff about being able to get children to go to bed so I captured the 6½ year old boy and carried him to his room. He is a nice boy, cheerful and mischievous like Tim, and it made me feel homesick.

2 June 1945. Saturday.
12 noon.
Last night the old Oxonians and Cantabrigians gave a dinner at
the University Club to everyone in S.F. who had been at either
university. It was most enjoyable. The best steak I have had since
Chicago at Flannagan's. Wilson of New Zealand told a good story
of a discussion in his committee of the preamble to the Charter. [J.
V. Wilson, Department of External Affairs of New Zealand.] The
draft contains Smut's phrase about "fratricidal strife." The Ukrai-
nian chairman of the Committee said that he could not bring
back to the Ukraine a document which said that the Germans
were brothers. Senator Rolin of Belgium [Lieutenant-Colonel
Henri Rolin] defended the use of the term on the Christian
ground of the brotherhood of all men and said that the fact that
Cain and Abel were brothers made Cain's crime the more odious.
The translator wearily in his translation referred to Abel killing
Cain. At this point the Soviet representative who was sitting beside Wilson turned to him in exasperation and said—"This
younger generation knows nothing about the scriptures." I got
off to my neighbours at dinner my suggestion for the title of an
essay on the Conference "Two Worlds: a sequel to Wendell Wilkie's 'One World.' " It was well received as well as the "per ardua ad cartam castratam" and "an expense of spirit in a waste of
shame." I also said I was going to propose a chapter at the end of
the Charter entitled, "Nothings in this Charter." It would repeat
all the articles in the Charter beginning with those words which
taken together make almost nothing of the Charter.

The news this morning from Scotty Reston is that the Soviet
reply on the veto is as bad as it could possibly be. It is more restrictive than the official U.S. interpretation of three or four months
ago. There is some fear that the Russians may be preparing the
way to a refusal to sign the Charter. I cannot believe it will come to
that. My guess is that what will probably happen is that the Yalta
veto formula will stand in its worst possible form and that in return for swallowing this bitter medicine the Conference will insist
that the Charter be valid for only ten years. The worst that I think
is likely to happen is that the Conference will sign no Charter but
will recess to meet again in Washington in say two months' time
in the expectation that in the interval the points at issue can be
resolved.

The history of this Conference will be written some day by

some brilliant historian. He will emphasize the ironies. One of
the bitterest of the ironies is that while the Conference was discussing trusteeship the French bombarded and bombed Damascus. It is a pity they did not see the light on the road to Damascus.
The incident has inflamed the Arabs; it has driven a wedge between the British and the French; it has driven the U.S. and the
U.K. closer together; and moved France away from the Atlantic
hemisphere to the Soviet hemisphere. The Russians are fishing in
troubled waters and will strengthen their position in the near and
middle east.

The atmosphere of the Coordination Committee is somewhat peculiar. We are guarded as if we were the chiefs of staff. The
meeting is held on the top floor of the Opera House, reached only
by one elevator. In order to get on that elevator you have to be
checked not only by the armed soldiers but by a civilian official. A
balcony lies off the Committee room and on this balcony a soldier
marches up and down on patrol while the Committee meets. I
give Norman all kinds of suggestions for improving the language
of the text. One of our redrafts of an article is now always called
"Mr. Robertson's draft." It was described by one member as "laconic" which he seemed to think was a fault. It read—"The original members of the Organization shall be the states which sign
and ratify the Charter." A half-hour debate took place on whether
this would not mean that, if the Organization never came into
effect because of the failure of sufficient states to join, states would
be members of the Organization even though there was no
Organization.

There were two occasions at the U.N. meetings I attended in
San Francisco and London when it looked as if the erosion of the
alliance between the western powers and the Soviet Union might
lead to a decision by the Soviet government not to join the U.N.
The first was at San Francisco early in June; the second in London
at the meetings of the Executive Committee in September and October. The crisis at San Francisco was over the extent of the veto
rights of the five permanent members of the Security Council.
The Soviet Union insisted on 1 June that any one of the permanent members should have the right to prevent the Security Council from discussing an international dispute.[11] The United States
government informed the Soviet government on 2 June that the

"United States could not possibly accept an Organization subject to such a restricted procedure . . ." and instructed Harry Hopkins, who was visiting Moscow, and Averill Harriman, the United States ambassador in Moscow, that "we will have to take the necessary steps to wind up the [San Francisco] conference here if we have nothing favorable from you in this regard."[12] The next day the Canadian delegation at San Francisco informed Ottawa that "we cannot exclude the possibility that [the Soviet Union] have decided that membership in the Organization will not be to their advantage."[13] Norman Robertson, the acting head of the Canadian delegation, informed the delegation on the following day that "it was on the whole a very disturbing deadlock, that had implications that went far beyond the Conference itself." On 7 June the Soviet government retreated from its demand and the crisis was over.

Gladwyn Jebb [later Lord Gladwyn] was an adviser on the British delegation to the San Francisco Conference and was later executive secretary of the Executive Committee and the Preparatory Commission. In his memoirs he says:

> Extraordinary though it may appear in retrospect . . . there was (apart from Poland) only one major crisis during the [San Francisco] conference when it looked as if it might possibly break up in confusion. This occurred on 2 June when after some five weeks of agitated debate, Gromyko flatly rejected the thesis that there should be an automatic obligation on the Security Council to discuss and consider *any* dispute duly brought to its attention: in other words an implicit demand by the Russians that they should have the right to veto even the discussion [by the Security Council] of any subject which seemed to them to be undesirable. . . . Gromyko insisted that "automaticity" was a retreat from the Crimea [the three-power Yalta agreement on the veto], and declared that the Soviet Union would not sign the Charter unless the principle were abandoned. . . . If Harry Hopkins never did anything else, he saved the San Francisco Conference by persuading Stalin to overrrule his subordinate.[14]

In this last statement Gladwyn Jebb was uncharacteristically careless in his language. Stalin did not overrule his subordinate. He changed his instructions. On a matter of this importance, and indeed at that time even on matters of minor importance, Gromyko always acted under instructions from Moscow. Adlai Stevenson, in a letter to his wife from the San Francisco Conference, said, "Poor Gromyko can't spit without permission from Moscow."[15]

4 June 1945. Monday.
4:40 p.m.
The news is so bad that it is unbelievable but perhaps the thing can be saved. It doesn't bear thinking about. . . . The latest crisis makes it impossible to say when the Conference is likely to be over. It might be wound up quickly or it may drag on in the hope of the big three reaching agreement on the veto. Everybody is in a blue state—Norman, Hume, Dana.

6 June 1945. Wednesday.
3:40 p.m.
I like living in the suite with Norman and Hume [which I had moved into a week before]. It gives me a chance to see more of them and to get to know them better. Norman is the better person in the kind of serious crisis the Conference—or rather the world— has been going through in the past week. His dislike of making a final decision one way or the other, of slamming doors shut, his phlegmatic qualities, which are often annoying weaknesses when he is dealing with small matters, are sources of strength in a real crisis. During the crisis I have been very glad that he was head of the delegation and not Hume. [Robertson had become head of the delegation a week or so before when all the politicians on the delegation had gone back to Canada to take part in the general election.] All this means of course that Norman and I are pretty much on the same side. My view is that once we are convinced that the Soviet Union is not bluffing when they say they will refuse to join the Organization if such and such a provision is in (or not in) we have to give in to them. Otherwise we precipitate the formation of two rival alliances. I was more or less accused of being an appeaser and being inconsistent but I was able to point out that this was the precise stand I had taken in my memorandum on the veto written three or four months ago. [In this memorandum of 16 March 1945, which I had sent to the Department of External Affairs, I had said:

The objective of Canadian policy should be to strive to the limit (the practical limit being the point at which the USSR would refuse to join the Organization) for [restrictions on the great power veto] to (1) expulsion of a permanent member or suspension of its veto right (2) imposition of a settlement on the parties to a dispute, by the threat or use of force (3) application of any form of sanction (4) ratification of a decision by a regional organization to apply any form of sanction.[16]]

Hume is much too ready to contemplate the immediate formation of two alliance systems. X [an officer of the Department] is dangerously irresponsible. He has twice said that, if there is to be a showdown with the Russians, it had better come before the German army is disbanded so that we can use it. I was able to have a chance to talk to Norman for about 15 minutes by himself on Monday morning on the crisis with the Soviets. I then put my argument in a one-page memorandum and at midnight argued pretty strongly in a discussion with Norman, Hume and X— Norman siding with me and Hume coming around a bit at the end.

Norman hasn't said anything to me about future plans and I'm not going to raise it till the very end of the Conference. It now looks as if an interim commission of the new Organization will be set up in London to function until the Organization comes into existence. If so we'll be a member and we'll have to have someone in London to sit on it. It would be an interesting job and my chances of getting it might be good if they don't give it to the High Commissioner (and suggest I do all the work but not get the prestige or credit). . . .

I have had to speak twice lately at meetings on the Secretariat. Both times it was essential to be as polite as possible to the Russians without receding from the report of a sub-committee which was based on our own amendments. Friday evening's session was the worst. The sub-committee had brought in a very slight revision of a four-power amendment. Unfortunately the U.S. which had been on the committee had forgotten to clear the report with the USSR. None of us knew that and the whole committee was taken aback when the Russians proposed that the committee take as its basis of discussion not the relevant paragraphs in the sub-committee's report but the original four-power amendment. This led to tremendous confusion and annoyance which reached its apex when the chairman, a very nice but not very effective foreign minister of Costa Rica, exploded and asked four rhetorical questions of the committee which could be paraphrased into—"Why in bloody hell should we go to drafting sub-committees and work until midnight preparing a revised text when we might be having fun going to dances or whatnot (loud cheers at this point) if the results of our labours are to be disregarded because of the bloody Russians."

I got up to pour oil on troubled waters. I said I felt sure that the long and painful debate had been due to an unhappy misunderstanding about the nature of the amendments which had been made by the drafting committee; that from the explanations made by other members of the committee it was now clear that no substantial changes had been made but that the language used by the great powers had been clarified and redundancies cut out; that members of the committee whose mother tongue was English or French were at an advantage in the committee and that I was sure there was not one member of the Committee who would not grant the Soviet delegation the courtesy of delaying the vote until the next session if they wanted more time to think it over. They then got up and accepted the sub-committee's draft.

Last night's session was however more grim. The final paragraph recommended by the sub-committee for the chapter on the Secretariat was one providing for the appointment of the staff by the Secretary-General under rules to be established by the Assembly; that the primary consideration to be taken into account was efficiency, competence and integrity, and the second consideration, equitable geographical distribution. The Soviets started the ball rolling by formally moving the suppression of the whole paragraph. The only encouraging thing in their remarks was the argument that technical matters of this character would "debase the value of the present Charter as the most important historical document of our time." A good debating point was that it was a reflection on the integrity of the Secretary-General since it assumed that without this provision he would appoint persons who were inefficient, incompetent or lacking in integrity. Paul Gore Booth was representing the U.K. and Harley Notter the U.S. Notter virtually refused to talk the matter over with me but I managed to get a word with Paul. Paul agreed that it would be useful if I pointed out that the USSR had already signed three agreements containing the very language they were now objecting to. I then spent an uneasy fifteen minutes trying to find a formula for putting the argument politely and not in such a way as to make the Soviet delegation look silly. Finally what I said was that the unanimity of the drafting committee in submitting the report was not accidental but arose out of the fact that the paragraph was based on similar provisions in other documents drawn up over the past two or three years by international conferences which had been participated in *not only by the five great powers* but by some forty of the other nations represented at the Conference. The Russians, however, stupidly refused to withdraw their proposal and were beaten 6:26. The committee text was then put to the vote and carried 30:3, the Russians getting only their own three votes: USSR, Byelorussia, and the Ukraine, with the other great powers abstaining.

The encouraging thing about the meeting was the responsibility of the members of the committee. They were scrupulously polite; lavish in praising the searching character of the Russian criticisms; and at the same time firm. It was as if the dying body of 19th century liberalism had decided to teach the powerful barbarian a lesson in good manners.

8 June 1945. Friday.
6:15 p.m.
Now that the crisis is over on the veto it is possible to make a guess as to when the conference will close. My guess is between the 22nd and the 25th. . . . While the conference may still have some hot arguments it is no longer possible that it will break down. The Russians have played their cards beautifully. Whether they planned it that way from the beginning, I don't know. They took an extreme position and then after precipitating a crisis retreated to something only a little less extreme. Now we are supposed to be (and in fact are) so grateful to them that we can do little but swallow under protest the old voting formula which is so repugnant.

The arrest of Kate Mitchell and some of the other I.P.R. [Institute of Pacific Relations] people and two men in the State Department is pretty terrible. They are being branded as spies when the most they did was to pass out or use information which should have been kept secret. But that is an offense which many government officials in Washington have been guilty of. Instead of arresting Kate they might have picked on people who have committed more flagrant and dangerous offences. My hope is that no jury will convict. Whatever happens, however, the I.P.R. is going to be smeared.

I am today the saviour of the big powers from an embarrassing situation. Representatives of the U.S. (Miss Gildersleeve), U.K. and France came up to me after the meeting to thank me for having saved the situation. Peru had moved with great publicity in the press a motion to include in the Charter a provision that save in exceptional circumstances all meetings of the Assembly should be open to the public and press of the world. It is the kind of thing which appropriately belongs in the rules to be adopted by the Assembly and each of the five great powers in turn got up this afternoon to oppose it on these grounds. It would have looked terrible if the motion of Peru were passed by a large majority with the big five in the negative. I moved a substitute motion that the committee recommend that the General Assembly at its first meeting include in its rules a provision that save in exceptional circumstances its meetings should be public. This enabled people to vote against the Peru motion on the ground that this was their only way to get a vote on my motion. The Peru motion was lost by 15:22 and mine carried by 34:0. The unanimity I was after was spoilt however because the Soviet delegate abstained and then, instead of staying silent, got up after the vote to explain that he abstained because a resolution incorporated in the rapporteur's report had no binding force unless ratified by the governments. Obviously the poor man had no instructions and was afraid to get in wrong with Moscow. . . .

The Coordination Committee has still not got really down to work but it is a good sign that tomorrow we begin meeting in the morning. Next week I imagine we'll be meeting six hours or more a day. I am cheered that, without my suggesting it, Norman proposed that we get the secretary of the Commission to circulate Canadian redrafts of two articles. If the experiment proves successful we may be able to circulate a large number. It is not very important except that it would be a pity if school children and university students had to study (and even memorize parts of) a document drawn up in barbaric English. Tomorrow morning we start on the preamble, principles and purposes. Norman suggested today that Archie MacLeish [Archibald MacLeish, librarian of Congress] rewrite them but apparently Leo Pasvolsky believes he is as great a master of English as MacLeish. However the seed has been planted and it may bear fruit. The thing is now terrible. All three sections—preamble, purposes and principles— end in an anti-climax. I scribbled on Norman's copy—"Not with a bang but a whimper." If the thing is not substantially improved I shall certainly never feel disgraced by the publication in parallel columns of the *Free World* draft of the corresponding sections and the San Francisco charter. [At a meeting of the United States delegation held the next day, 9 June, Dean Virginia C. Gildersleeve reported that she was in a difficult position in respect to the preamble. Some one had submitted to the press the draft of the preamble agreed to by the committee and had attributed it to Smuts and herself. She declared that, as a professor of English, she protested against having this draft attributed to her. Pašvolsky assured her that the Coordination Committee would revise the preamble.[17]]

9 June 1945. Saturday.
10:30 p.m.
This has been an easy day for me. I went to a Coordination Committee this morning with Norman, for a walk in Golden Gate Park this afternoon with Gordon Robertson and dinner tonight with Chipman and Gordon. At the moment I am a bit befuddled due to two whiskeys before dinner and a bottle of wine at dinner. The California wine is very good. . . . At dinner Chipman, Gordon and I were discussing the difficulties of drafting the Charter with Sir William Malkin, the U.K. legal adviser. We were making fun of some of the platitudes and obscurities in the text. At the end of dinner an American from the next table came over and protested against us treating lightly the sacred objectives which we (the American people) had in mind. Oh hell!

12 June 1945. Tuesday.
Midnight.
Have a good time at Mark's [Marquis Childs's] and give Mark and Biddy my love. Tell Mark I still haven't completely given up hope of our being able to live out the rest of our life without being bombed but keeping the bombs away is going to be a long, dreary job requiring better nerves and more intelligence and politeness than we now seem to possess.

19 June 1945. Tuesday.
4:00 p.m.
I am terribly sorry to have gone so long without writing you but life has been pretty grim lately. The Coordination Committee has been working from ten in the morning until midnight; we have a delegation meeting at 9:15 every morning and after midnight Norman and I go over the work of the day. I am feeling sleepy but otherwise all right. I am writing this at a meeting of the Coordination Committee which is going over muddy ground we have gone over about four times already. We made our fight on it about two weeks ago and are now lying back on our oars and letting the UK and the USSR do the work of trying to cut useless repetitions out of the Charter. . . .

What my future will be after the Conference I don't know. The job in London on the interim Executive Committee will be pretty well a full-time job until the first meeting of the Assembly a year or so from now. My chances of getting the job are, I think, pretty good since, as a result of sitting in at the Coordination Committee, I know more about the meaning of the Charter than anyone else except Norman. I would rather be invited to take the job than ask for it so I am waiting for Norman to make the first move.

My admiration for Norman increases constantly. He is, I imagine, at his best at a meeting of about the size of this Coordination Committee—fourteen. He makes his points firmly and effectively except occasionally when he mutters a laconic and penetrating comment which is consequently lost until sometimes he brings it up again half an hour later in a louder voice.

Last night we had a small dinner in a private room at the hotel to try to revise the bloody preamble which is now unutterably bad. We had Archie MacLeish, Bailey (Australia), Jebb (UK), Gilson (a famous French professor of medieval studies), and Georges Demolin (the chief adviser to the international secretariat of the Conference on the French translation). [Professor K. H. Bailey, Attorney General's Department, Canberra. Etienne Gilson, professor at the Collège de France.] We drank, ate a very good dinner, talked and drank from 7:30 to 12:30 and finally produced something which was not a masterpiece but three times as good as the one approved by the technical committee which was a mutilated version of an original written by Smuts in March and added to by C. K. Webster. We were all very proud of ourselves but, in order to avoid a row, Norman called on Smuts this morning and the old fool refused to give our new draft his blessing. So now we are where we began except tireder and more discouraged. . . .

It is now 5:30. The Committee is moving very slowly since all its members are pretty well drunk with fatigue. Poor Pasvolsky (the chairman) is the most tired of all but never shows impatience. Every little while, however, his mind begins to run a bit slow. (6:15) No time for more. Norman may be turning his chair over to me soon to bring forward some ideas on the peaceful settlement chapter.

The following day, 20 June, I learned that my wife was not well and I flew back to Washington. The Charter was signed on 26 June, five days after I left San Francisco. My wife, our three children, and I went to Canada expecting to return to the Washington embassy in September, but while I was working in Ottawa in the second half of July writing a draft of the Canadian report on the San Francisco Conference, I was appointed to the Canadian delegation to the Executive Committee of the Preparatory Commission, which was to meet in London in August, and I sailed to England at the beginning of August. I was told that the intention of the Department was that I would be appointed to the staff of the Canadian High Commission in London and that my family would join me in London in September. By the end of September this seemed improbable but it was not until the beginning of November that I was informed that, instead of being appointed to London, I would be posted to the Department of External Affairs in Ottawa. (My guess now is that the Canadian high commissioner in London, Vincent Massey, did not want me on his staff.) I hoped that I would be back in Ottawa before Christmas but it was decided that I should remain in London for the meeting of the General Assembly in January in order to provide continuity with the work of the Executive Committee and the Preparatory Commission.

I was disappointed at the time in not being appointed to the High Commission in London but I now know that this was a providential happening. If I had been in London for the usual term of four years from 1945 to, say, 1949, I would not have been able to exercise the influence I did on Canadian policy in the U.N.

in 1946 and 1947, or to work hand-in-hand with Pearson on the making of the North Atlantic Treaty from 1947 to 1949. Moreover, working directly under Pearson in Ottawa from 1946 on resulted in Pearson giving me rapid promotion until, in 1948, I was second-in-command of the Department. My thanks are due to Vincent Massey for vetoing my appointment to London in 1945.

I prepared my draft of the Canadian report on the San Francisco Conference in Ottawa during nine days in July 1945. It was about 30,000 words long. A great deal of it, perhaps the greater part, did not appear in the final printed report.[18] I had tried to make the report interesting and intelligible, and not like the dry-as-dust reports which the Department of External Affairs had published on the meetings of the League of Nations. It was not until Pearson took over the direction of the Department and Robertson went to London as high commissioner and Wrong to Washington as ambassador that I succeeded in writing and having published what I considered to be the right kind of report. When this report on the U.N. General Assembly held in New York in the autumn of 1946[19] appeared, Norman Smith began his two-column article on it on the editorial page of the *Ottawa Journal* on 2 April 1947 as follows:

> The Department of External Affairs, of all places, has scoffed at tradition and presented a report to Parliament based on the assumption that it will be read. . . . Written in the most fastidious English, presented in good type, the Department's story of U.N. is helpfully comprehensive but not overwhelming. . . . [Reading this report] is like drawing up a chair with one of the Department's experts for a three-hour talk.

I give below four passages from my draft of the report of the San Francisco Conference which did not appear in the final printed version: preamble, enforcement arrangements, the accomplishment of the Conference, and the task before us. The last passage was probably considered too rhetorical. It was not, however, wasted. I kept in those days a folder of what I considered to be the best of such rejected passages—passages which I had written for speeches and statements and which had not been used. At the General Assembly in New York on 4 December 1946 I was asked to write a speech on disarmament for the head of the delegation to give four hours later at a plenary meeting of the Assembly. I had in the preceding three days written two speeches for him for plenary meetings. I was out of ideas. I had recourse to a stiff drink of whiskey and to my folder of rejections and dictated a speech consisting at least in half of rejections. One of the rejections I used, with minor changes, was "The task before us." The speech was warmly received by the Assembly. A member of the American delegation who admired it said to me that he was, however, puzzled that at several places in the speech he thought it was about to come to an end. I did not tell him that this was because it contained three perorations.

Preamble
The preamble is based on a draft drawn up by Field-Marshal Smuts. It is an integral part of the Charter, although the precise obligations of the member states are indicated in the succeeding chapters. The preamble can be briefly paraphrased as follows. [I called this a paraphrase but it was in fact the preamble which most members of the Coordination Committee wanted but failed to get accepted.]

> We, the peoples of the United Nations, believe in the worth and dignity of the individual, in the rule of law and justice among nations and in respect for the pledged word. We are persuaded that men and nations can by their joint and sustained efforts live together as good neighbours free from fear and want and with liberty of thought and worship. We are resolved to save ourselves and our children from the scourge of war which twice in our time has brought us untold loss and sorrow. Therefore we unite our strength to keep the peace.

Enforcement Arrangements[20]
[This was a comment on the Dumbarton Oaks proposals on enforcement arrangements. These proposals were not altered in essential matters at the San Francisco Conference.]
When the Dumbarton Oaks proposals were first published, public attention was concentrated on that section of the proposals which subsequently became Chapter VII of the Charter. This was the section providing for the use of the combined forces of the Members of the Organization against a troublemaking state. The

section, however, had to be read along with the section on voting procedure in the Security Council which emerged from the Yalta Conference. Under this proposed voting procedure any one of the five great powers could veto the use of the whole of the section giving the Organization teeth. This meant that the Organization could not use force against a great power or against any other state which any one of the great powers wanted to shield. The use of the teeth of the Organization was limited not only by the Yalta voting formula but also by the Dumbarton Oaks proposals on transitional arrangements. It was apparent from these proposals that the Organization's teeth were not to be used against ex-enemy states. Thus, on examination, it became clear that, under the Dumbarton Oaks proposals, force, whether economic or armed, could be brought to bear by the Organization only against those middle or small powers which had either been neutral in the war or which had been members of the victorious coalition and which no great power wished to shield against the imposition of sanctions. The actual use of force under the Dumbarton Oaks proposals was thus a remote contingency since the mere willingness of all the great powers to use force would, in the twentieth century as in past centuries, ordinarily be sufficient to bring any conceivable combination of middle and small powers to heel. In spite of this, to dismiss the enforcement section of the Dumbarton Oaks proposals as unimportant would have been unrealistic and superficial. In course of time the Organization would assume responsibility for preventing renewed acts of aggression by the ex-enemy states, and this would be a serious responsibility. Moreover the Charter to be constructed on the basis of the Dumbarton Oaks proposals was to be a beginning and not an end. It was to be the foundation of a new structure to create and preserve peace, not the whole vast completed edifice. If the Organization was to free the peoples of the world from the fear of war it would eventually have to be given the right and the power to restrain any disturber of the world's peace.

The Accomplishment of the Conference

The San Francisco Conference gave birth to a charter of a world peace league of which all the great powers would be members. This was its accomplishment. The Charter of the United Nations is not a perfect document. Like the constitution of the United States and other great historic documents it contains evasions, compromises and ambiguities. But its value is not to be found from a meticulous examination of its text. Its value resides in its potentialities. The Charter of the United Nations, if properly used by the governments and peoples of the world, can be what it is intended to be—the foundation of a just and stable world order in which men may be able to achieve freedom from fear and from want, freedom of thought and of worship. It is possible to compare the Charter clause by clause with the Covenant of the League of Nations and to draw up a balance sheet showing on one side of the ledger where the Charter is better than the Covenant and on the other side of the ledger where it is not as good. That is a useful thing to do but the importance of the results should not be exaggerated. The Charter of the United Nations is better than the Covenant because of one simple fact: the United States was never a member of the League, the Soviet Union was a member for only five years; both the United States and the Soviet Union are going to be members of the United Nations from its very beginning. They, along with the United Kingdom and China, conceived it at Dumbarton Oaks; they saw it through its labour pains at San Francisco; it is their child, fashioned in their image. They possess the legal right to subject the child to unnecessary restrictions and prohibitions during its first years when its character is being formed; they can give it too little to feed on; they can disregard it; they can refuse to give it the responsibilities without which it cannot grow in wisdom and in stature; by so doing they can stunt and warp its growth and prevent it from ever becoming a mature and responsible adult. The great powers can do all this because they possess great power. They have the legal right to do it under the veto provisions of the Charter. But to assume that they would do it is to assume that they were acting in bad faith when they drew up the Charter and persuaded the rest of the United Nations to accept it and that they do not believe that the creation, preservation and strengthening of the Organization serve the interests of their peoples. Such an assumption is baseless.

The Task Before Us
The San Francisco Conference, by reaching agreement on the Charter of the United Nations, laid the foundation of a just and stable world order in which men may be able to achieve freedom

from fear and from want, freedom of thought and of worship. The representatives of Canada at the Conference played a part in that undertaking. They hope that the people of Canada will feel that the part they played was not unworthy of the losses and sufferings which the men, women and children of Canada have undergone in two world wars. San Francisco laid the foundation of a new world order. That was a great accomplishment but it is only a beginning. It is the task of the living generation of men to strengthen that foundation and to build on it a great structure. The task will be heavy. It will be long and dreary. It will be full of set-backs and heart-breaks. There will be periods of joy but there will also be periods of despair. Some parts of the foundation, some bits of the structure, will turn out to be badly planned or badly constructed and will collapse. Other bits will need to be shored up. If we, the peoples of the United Nations, are to succeed in our task we must be willing to experiment, and to run great risks to attain great objections. We must be resolute and display in our just cause a holy obstinacy. We must have faith in ourselves and in each other. Above all we must remember that all men are brothers and that upon the dignity, the liberty, the inviolability of the individual men, women and children of the world depend the welfare of the people, the safety of the state, and the peace of the world.

27 July 1945. Friday.
Chateau Laurier, Ottawa.
My private hope is six to one that I shall be given the job of second-in-command at [the High Commission in] London and that we shall be seeing each other again in two months. . . .

The English election results are really wonderful. [The victory of the Labour party.] My black guess about the future used to be that another great war in twenty-five years was a four to one chance. My hope is that it is now two to one. I'm sure it is going to make the work in London [on the Executive Committee of the Preparatory Commission] much easier and more fruitful. It's conceivable that Noel-Baker might be the U.K. representative but whoever it is he will push for liberalizing the [U.N.] Charter by adopting the best possible rules and regulations. [P. J. Noel-Baker, Labour M.P., was appointed minister of state in the Foreign Office and chief U.K. delegate to the Executive Committee.]

The mere being in London for the first six months of a real Labour government will be vastly exciting. I do hope they try hard to carry out their promises fast.

1 August 1945.
1:45 p.m.
En route Montreal to Quebec.
I spent a very pleasant hour with Mr. [H.J.] Symington at his office this morning. He stayed over to see me. He looks the same as ever. I think he has taken refuge [from the pain of the death of his son in action in the last days of the war in Europe] in his mission to try to lessen international friction by building up the [international civil] air convention to the place where we failed to build it at Chicago. . . . I am very fond of him. . . . Most [of the passengers on this boat train] . . . are English children returning home.

7 August 1945. Tuesday.
S.S. Stratheden.
I am in despair today about the kind of world our children are going to live in. I have hoped against hope until today that the atomic bomb would not be discovered. Now all the vistas of Titanic glooms of chasmed fears open up. . . . I just haven't enough faith in man or god to believe that we have enough time or intelligence or goodwill to reach the goal of a world government before we obliterate civilization in another war. But there's nothing to do except to live as if it were possible, and to try one's best to make it possible.

I wrote Mother before I sailed and in my letter said that I thought I suffered from a sense of guilt because I had not fought in either of the wars and that it was because of that that I was unsuccessfully trying to sacrifice my constitution in the fight for peace. The explanation is too simple but there's something in it. What I don't want to do is to sacrifice your happiness and that of the children to salve my uneasy conscience. I've done too much of that already. I'll try to work out some better modus vivendi. Now that we're in for a long pull until we're dead perhaps I can resolve the conflict by leading a less tense and therefore, in the long run, a more effective life. During the last nine months I've learned a lot about how to conquer my only disease—nervous tension. If I can make time in which to enjoy companionship with you and the children perhaps I can conquer it altogether and at the same time make life happier for you and Patrick and Morna and Timothy. Don't think I have been worrying about this all this trip. I haven't. I've been trying to let my mind lie fallow. But the holiday has, I think, given me time to pause between two worlds—the pre-atomic and the post-atomic.

4
The Executive Committee
16 AUGUST–27 OCTOBER 1945

The Executive Committee of the Preparatory Commission met in London from 16 August to 27 October 1945. It drew up recommendations for the fifty-nation Preparatory Commission which met in London from 24 November to 23 December. It and the Preparatory Commission were established by an agreement on interim arrangements which was signed in San Francisco on 26 June by the nations which had that day signed the Charter.[1] In this agreement the Executive Committee and the Preparatory Commission were instructed to "prepare the provisional agenda for the first sessions of the principal organs of the Organization, and [to] prepare documents and recommendations relating to all matters on these agenda." The Charter had established six principal organs: the General Assembly, the Security Council, the Economic and Social Council, the Trusteeship Council, the International Court of Justice, and the Secretariat. The Executive Committee and the Preparatory Commission were also instructed to make recommendations on the location of the permanent headquarters of the U.N. The two bodies therefore drew up a mass of recommendations which included a recommendation on the location of the U.N. headquarters; draft rules of procedure for the General Assembly and the Councils; regulations on the Secretariat; financial regulations; proposals on the structure of the Assembly, the Economic and Social Council, and the Secretariat; the language rules for the Assembly; a resolution on trusteeship; and a convention on the privileges, immunities, and facilities to be accorded to the U.N. by its members. In a memorandum I wrote at the conclusion of the Executive Committee's work I said that the U.N. Charter was similar to a written national constitution. A written national constitution had to be supplemented by constitutional statutes. "The job of the Preparatory Commission is to prepare the constitutional statutes to supplement the constitution."

The Executive Committee prepared a detailed report to the Preparatory Commission. The Commission made a number of substantial changes in the Executive Committee's recommendations and submitted them to the General Assembly, the Security Council, and the other organs of the U.N. The General Assembly met in London from 10 January to 14 February 1946 and adopted the recommendations with little change.

In London at the Executive Committee I found myself working with colleagues I had worked with in San Francisco on the Coordination Committee: Gladwyn Jebb of Britain, who had become executive secretary of the Executive Committee and the Preparatory Commission, (Alger Hiss had held the corresponding position at the San Francisco Conference.), C. K. Webster of Britain, Paul Hasluck of Australia, Cyro de Freitas-Valle of Brazil, and Adrian Pelt of the Netherlands. These had been among the most constructive members of the Coordination Committee. I was particularly happy that Hasluck was my Australian colleague. I, like him, look back on our association in the Executive Committee and the Preparatory Commission as a "pleasant feature of my work." Our close association was made easier by the accidents of the alphabet which put us close to each other at meetings and, as he puts it in his memoirs, "we became what in those days was called 'a ginger group,' throwing up many suggestions which some other delegates thought were good ideas."[2]

The victory of the Labour party in the general election in Britain which took place shortly after the San Francisco Conference strengthened British representation since it resulted in Philip Noel-Baker becoming the chief British delegate. This made my task easier and more pleasant since I had known Noel-Baker and liked and respected him ever since we first met at the unofficial British Commonwealth Relations Conference in Toronto in 1933, which I had helped to organize as the national secretary of the Canadian Institute of International Affairs.

Stettinius was unfortunately the chief United States delegate to the Executive Committee but Adlai Stevenson was his second-in-command and took over from him in the middle of October when Stettinius had to return to the United States because of illness. The delegation of China was headed by two experienced diplomats, Wellington Koo and Victor Hoo, but China contributed little to the meetings of the ten subcommittees of the Executive Committee.

The Executive Committee, London, September 1945. From left to right, on the far side of the table are Luis Padilla Nervo, Mexico; J. H. van Roijen, Netherlands; A. A. Gromyko, USSR; P. J. Noel-Baker, U.K.; and E. R. Stettinius, U.S.A. Escott Reid sits opposite Stettinius.

Much the same was true of the French delegation which was headed
by René Massigli, the French ambassador in London. Czechoslovakia and Yugoslavia, because of their susceptibility to Soviet pressure, had limited freedom of action. Iran was represented by Nasrul-
lah Entezam, a former minister of foreign affairs. Part of Iran was at
the time occupied by the Soviet Union and the crisis between Iran
and the Soviet Union was mounting, but Entezam showed no
signs in his speeches or votes of being intimidated by the Soviet
Union. He displayed heartening personal and political courage.
Luis Padilla Nervo of Mexico was an able representative. The
Netherlands delegation was greatly strengthened by the appointment of Herman van Roijen as chief delegate. Andrei Gromyko
headed the Soviet delegation, ably assisted by Alexei A. Roschin.[3]

As in San Francisco, so in London, Gromyko was given little
or no latitude by the Soviet government. He was told how he was to
vote. He was seldom told the reasons he should give to explain his
vote. This resulted in his delivering the following sort of speech
time after time: "The Soviet delegation has studied carefully the
amendment proposed by the delegation of A to the proposed rule X
of the rules of procedure of the General Assembly [or some other
organ]. In the opinion of the Soviet delegation the proposed
amendment would not improve the rule of procedure. The Soviet
delegation believes that rule X is a very good rule. Therefore the
Soviet delegation will vote against the amendment proposed by the
delegation of A."

Sometimes, of course, errors or delays in interpreting from the
working languages (English and French) into Russian were a bar to
understanding. At one time a long confused debate in the Executive
Committee went on into the early hours of the morning with Gromyko using every possible device to prevent the adoption of a resolution which he had been opposing for weeks. Finally Gromyko
indicated that he would no longer oppose the taking of a vote
(where he knew he would be defeated) if the views of the Soviet
delegation were set forth fully in the protocol. Stettinius, who was
in the chair, was baffled; he said there was no protocol. The debate
dragged on. Finally I saw the light. I said: "Mr. Chairman. It seems
to me that what Mr. Gromyko means by the protocol are the minutes of our meeting." Gromyko said that that was, of course, what
he meant. Stettinius assured him that his opposition would be set

forth fully in the minutes and we took the vote. What Gromyko needed was an official document to send to Moscow which would demonstrate that he had fought as hard as he possibly could to defeat a proposal which Moscow disliked.

Much of my work on the Executive Committee was exasperating and frustrating but most of it was exciting and constructive. When two weeks after its final meeting I was able to look back on it in some tranquillity, I wrote to my son, Patrick:

> Looking back at the Executive Committee's work, it went off very well. . . . The kind of work we have been doing . . .— rules of procedure, staff regulations, financial structure, committee structure, etc.,—may be of more permanent value than the Charter. The atomic bomb and other new weapons of war make necessary a much tighter union of the world than the Charter provides which is little more than an alliance plus a system for holding periodic conferences. If we don't get a tighter union we'll all be blown up.

16 August 1945. Thursday.
5:00 p.m.
London.

I had dinner on Tuesday night with Freitas-Valle at Claridges. He has a suite there which costs him 8 guineas [8 pounds, 8 shillings] a day and consists mostly of doors and cupboards and entrances. I waited till the eleven o'clock news but we were both too sleepy to stay up for a promised announcement at midnight. Consequently the first I heard of the surrender [of Japan] was when I picked up the *Daily Telegraph* outside my room at 7:45 in the morning. . . .

I spent most of yesterday (the first V.J. day) in my office trying to prepare some memoranda for the first meeting of the Executive Committee today. The morning was grey, cold and drizzly but the crowds were packed waiting for the royal procession. (I look out of my office which is the penthouse of Canada House over the whole of Trafalgar Square.) Then the crowds began to get more happy as the sun came out and the square was filled with moving people. They seemed cheerful. Some enthusiasts were dancing in circles or in pairs. Others climbed up to and into the fountain. Two put on a really good clown act falling repeatedly into the water. . . . After dinner John Holmes' party which by now included a tough drunken corporal—a friend of Doug LePan's—gathered again on the first balcony of Canada House overlooking the square and encouraged the promiscuous osculation going on below. [John W. Holmes and Douglas V. LePan, secretaries at the Canadian High Commission in London.] Any attractive unaccompanied woman was liable to be seized in a lasting embrace by any man in uniform. . . . John and I walked through Trafalgar Square about 10 p.m., saw a mass of humanity all the way down Whitehall, made our way to Leicester Square, gave up at the sight of Piccadilly Circus. Then I walked by myself through the Green Park to Buckingham Palace and so to my hotel. The crowd in front of the palace chanted every little while—"We want the King." I stayed a few minutes and then left. He came out shortly after. A curious people. So well-behaved. No rioting. Virtually no destruction. Just happily milling about cold sober with fathers carrying little children pick-a-back so that they could tell their great-grandchildren that they had seen the victory celebrations.

Freddie Hudd is a terrible Tory snob but he backs away from his views if you push him just a bit. [Frederick Hudd, second-in-command at the Canadian High Commission.] He came back from the opening of parliament with a Labour Minister and repeated with scorn and putting on a slight cockney accent the Minister's remark which was something like—"Let the poor people enjoy themselves for two days. They don't know how grim a time they are in for during the next few years." He thought it was terrible for a Labour Minister to say such a thing.

The first meeting of the Executive Committee went off all right this morning. [Philip] Noel-Baker [minister of state in the Foreign Office] is as charming as ever. He is now 55. He still has his hair but it is grey. He was most friendly and introduced me to Mr. [Ernest] Bevin [British foreign secretary] as an old friend. He was a most adroit chairman but refuses to continue as chairman since the Executive Secretary of the Committee (Gladwyn Jebb) is English. We are going to eat together soon. Even Jebb who is somewhat of a cold fish calls him "lovable." [In his memoirs Jebb called Noel-Baker "the saintly and well-disposed."[4]]

I've moved from my guinea [a day] cell at the Dorchester to a good-sized room in an old-fashioned family hotel, "Fords," on Manchester Street, two blocks from the Wallace Collection.

18 August 1945. Sunday.
Saul Rae [of the Department of External Affairs] is in town. He arrived yesterday. We had lunch together and afterwards took a bus to the east end to see the bomb damage. I said to the bus conductor that we wanted to see the docks. We ended up near the greyhound racing because he thought we said we wanted to go to the dogs. However we went through a lot of bombed areas out in Hackney. It was always pretty grim out there and it's worse now.

22 August 1945. Wednesday.
One thing which relieves an otherwise sombre outlook is that the atomic bomb was so revolutionary that even the thickest-headed realizes that a revolution has taken place to which we have to re-adjust all our thinking on international political organization. As soon as the bomb fell all the security articles in the Charter became archaic.

We are still going through the toils of organizing ourselves on the Executive Committee and getting to know each other. It now looks as if the sub-committees will not be able to get down to work till the middle of next week. We are now going through the terms of reference of the sub-committees but have had to take up a good deal of time on whether to let the press into our meetings. The Russians of course want to keep them at arms' length. Baker wants them in all the time. The U.S. is more on the Russian than the U.K. side. Mike [Pearson] couldn't come this morning so it fell to me to propose a compromise which went through. It has the merit of satisfying neither Baker nor the Russians. . . . It looks as if the working members of the full committee are going to be the big five and Australia, Brazil and Canada. The Australian representative, Paul Hasluck, who is about thirty-five and is in the External Affairs Department at Canberra, is turning out to be very good—much better than at San Francisco where I imagine he suffered from too minute a direction from Evatt.

Last night I took Freitas-Valle to dinner at the Greek restaurant where Noel-Baker had given me lunch—the Akropolis. . . . The other guest at Baker's lunch was Stephen Spender [English poet whom I had known at Oxford] whom I think I would have recognized even after fifteen years. I think he has become a thoroughly pleasant person and very intelligent. He has kind, sad eyes. He married about two years ago a Russian girl and they have a baby. Stephen is off to a series of visits to Germany for the British Government. He has already made one or two visits and Baker was much impressed by his reports. . . .

The prices of meals in restaurants vary very greatly. The Soho restaurants are five or six shillings [for dinner]. The luxury restaurants ten shillings with extras which make the total about twelve shillings. My hotel charges me five shillings for dinner and 3/6 for lunch. . . . A Scotch at a bar or restaurant costs five shillings or more. . . . But as long as [Vincent] Massey stays away I can give my dinner guests drinks [in his palatial office in Canada House] at about $1.60 a bottle for Seagrams V.O.

24 August 1945. Friday.
5:40 p.m.
The sub-committees are still not set up. We hold on Monday our first meeting which will be open to the press and hope then to adopt terms of reference for the sub-committees. The Russians now are creating difficulties about the temporary secretariat of the Committee. They clearly want it composed of officials seconded by the various delegations with no outsiders appointed. Baker was not at the meeting this morning and they scored a temporary victory but I think we can and must beat them on Monday. Their idea seems to be that an international secretariat is to be composed of nobody but stenographers and administrative officials. Life with the Russians is difficult but life without them would be impossible.

29 August 1945. Wednesday.
10:00 p.m.
Mike [Pearson] left this afternoon for a three-day flying trip to the Netherlands and Germany and he is flying back to Ottawa on Saturday. [Pearson had been appointed to represent Canada at the opening meetings of the Executive Committee.] So I am left alone as the captain and the mate and the crew and the cabin boy. My title is now "Acting Chief Delegate" and I get the invitations to the lunches at which most of the other guests are ambassadors. I had my first today at the Chilean Embassy where my neighbours were a Persian excellency who was very nice and fortunately could speak English as well as French, and an old friend of mine from San Francisco, [Adrian] Pelt, of the Netherlands Delegation. To-

morrow I lunch at the Chinese Embassy on the invitation of Wellington Koo, the Chinese Ambassador. We are still bogged down in the main committee so the sub-committees are still not set up. I sent Ottawa a telegram yesterday saying that the most pessimistic estimates of the duration of the committee's sessions were now justified. Don't pass this on but I think that the city which now has the best chance of being the seat of the Organization is San Francisco. It would be a lovely place to live in so keep your fingers crossed.

3 September 1945. Monday.
9:15 p.m.
Mike Pearson has gone off carrying my first long interpretative despatch, entitled "The first fortnight." It's about 2500 words long and isn't too bad. I'm going to try to write an interpretative despatch every fortnight to supplement the hurried brief communications. Noel-Baker is optimistic about getting the seat of the Organization in Geneva—the Swiss ceding Ariana and the French a piece of neighbouring territory to form an international city. . . .

Yesterday I spent most of the day saying good-bye to Mike. John Holmes, Alison Grant, Mary Gray and I had lunch with him at the Churchill Club, then met him again at six and saw him off at Euston at 8:30. Then we went back to the small house in Chelsea where the two girls live and had a very good supper with them cooked by a former member of the French underground, a boy who looks about twenty and was in a bad German concentration camp from which he was liberated by the Russian advance. His worst stories about the camp had to do with how the prisoners mistreated each other—the oldest inhabitants or the strongest, e.g. German political prisoners or Poles, beating up the newcomers and stealing from them. The first town near Berlin which he saw just after the Russians captured it had not a German in it and the Russians were mostly drunk and trying to ride the bicycles which the Germans had left behind—bicycles being unknown in Russia.

3 September 1945.
To the Department of External Affairs.[5]
Now that the Executive Committee has gone into subcommittee and has thus finished the first stage of its work it might

be useful if I were to make some general comments on developments in the Committee during the first two weeks of its existence.

No penthouse meetings

The most significant development is that there are no penthouse meetings [of the five great powers] taking place as at San
Francisco [where there were twenty-nine between 7 May and 21
June.] So far as I am aware the only joint recommendation which
has been made to the Executive Committee by the five great powers was on the acceptance by the Committee of the principle of a
rotating chairmanship. On the other questions which have come
before the Committee the five great powers do not appear to have
had any previous consultation and each has demonstrated its
freedom in committee to differ from the other great powers.

The Executive Committee, during the past two weeks, has
been dealing with a number of questions which have been
charged with political and emotional content, such as the nature
of the secretariat, relations with the League and relations with the
press. The fact that on such matters the five great powers have not
considered it wise nor useful to agree on a common line may
lessen our fears that they will present the Security Council with
agreed decisions on all important matters on its agenda.

It is too early, however, from the mere experience of two
weeks' work in a committee dealing with organizational questions to forecast what the attitude of the great powers will be on
the Security Council. I have a feeling that to some extent the attitude they have taken to date on the Executive Committee results
from Mr. Noel-Baker's strong personal distaste for secret five-
power conclaves. Some of the members of the British Delegation
have already privately referred to him as the chief spokesman of
the small powers. Now that Mr. Stettinius has arrived in London,
Mr. Stettinius' influence may be thrown in the direction of five-
power consultation. [Stettinius and his deputy, Adlai Stevenson,
had arrived in London on 1 September.]

[Stettinius's influence was indeed thrown in the direction of
five-power consultation and he had for a time the support of Ernest Bevin. According to Stettinius, Bevin, some time in September,
overruled Noel-Baker's objections to five-power meetings and
encouraged Stettinius "to go ahead and have five-power ex-
changes of views which he thought would be helpful." By 20 Jan-

uary 1946 Bevin had changed his mind. At an informal five-power meeting that day Bevin said, "I wish to make clear that while I am willing to have an informal exchange of views I cannot be committed to anything in this room. My Government must always be free to act according to its conscience." Stettinius in his report of this meeting went on to say,

> Later on in the afternoon he [Bevin] put it stronger, saying he disliked the five power consultations and hoped we would not have to have them often as it was bad to have secret conferences and would cause resentment in the United Nations.[6]]

Personnel of the Committee

The Executive Committee is, on the whole, a stronger committee than the Co-ordination Committee at San Francisco. Its most influential member is Mr. Noel-Baker. During the Coalition Government he had the task of dealing with the question of war transport which could not have been very close to his heart. Now that he is back with his old love again—collective security—he is bubbling over with ideas and enthusiasm. Because of his years in the wilderness he comes to his task much less jaded than most of the other members of the Committee.

Mr. [Benjamin] Gerig, the temporary chief of the United States delegation in Mr. Stettinius' absence, has presented his brief very ably but leaves the impression sometimes that he is not very enthusiastic about his brief. [Gerig, associate chief of the division of international organization affairs and chief of the division of dependent area affairs in the State Department.] In private conversation he frankly states that he is embarrassed by the voluminous and detailed instructions on every point on the agenda, which he receives every day from Mr. Pasvolsky and Mr. Dunn in Washington, and like so many United States civil servants he does not mind stating bluntly in private the points on which he disagrees with his instructions. He regrets, for example, the line taken by his people in Washington that the Executive Committee, being in their opinion, an agent of the embryo General Assembly, should keep its hands off the sacred great power organ—the Security Council—and though he has not been very precise in talking to me about the problem of the seat of the Organization, I am fairly certain that he himself is in favour of the seat being established at Geneva and not in the United States.

Mr. Gromyko is bound even more tightly by his instructions than Mr. Gerig. If it were not for the Soviet delegation the Executive Committee could probably have completed, in three days, what it has actually taken two weeks to do. (Indeed were it not for the Soviet Union the Committee might never have come into existence since the other powers at San Francisco would probably have been willing to appoint a temporary secretary-general and give him authority to make the necessary preparations for the first meetings of the organs of the Organization.) Mr. Gromyko gives the impression that he follows the letter of his instructions rather than their spirit and he has sorely tried the patience of the Committee by his stubborn refusal to admit defeat and by his insistence on raising again and again questions which have already been determined by the Committee against Soviet wishes. On this Committee the prime diplomatic virtue required is patience.

The difficulties which the Committee has encountered in dealing with the Soviet delegation may sometimes arise not out of Mr. Gromyko's stubbornness but out of his lack of command of English and French. At one meeting the other day the Committee, for example, made it clear at least three times that the Executive Secretary could appoint senior members of his secretariat from outside the ranks of officials of the fourteen countries represented on the Committee. I am fairly certain, however, that Mr. Gromyko still does not understand that this decision has been made.

As at San Francisco some of the difficulties in dealing with the Soviet delegation arise from the fact that the Soviet members do not understand what is meant by certain western political concepts. The idea of a civil service, whether national or international, which tries its best to be impartial and which, nevertheless of necessity, is concerned with the framing of policy as well as with the carrying out of government decisions, seems to be utterly foreign to them. They appear unable to distinguish between referring a proposal to a sub-committee for study and report and deciding in favour of the principle of a proposal. To them the two things are identical.

Dr. [V. K. Wellington] Koo, the chief of the Chinese delegation, has not, so far, had a chance to indicate his strength as a participant in discussions on questions of substance. As chairman he has, instead, done his best to avoid open differences of opinion in the Committee and to gloss over differences by finding a formula, even though the formula is so imprecise that it only postpones a decision on a question of substance, and may make it necessary for the battle to be fought all over again in all ten sub-committees.

The Australian delegate, Mr. Hasluck, has been one of the most useful members of the Committee and has demonstrated much more ability in London than he did in San Francisco. Perhaps the value of his contribution to an international discussion increases as the square of his distance from Dr. Evatt. He has been given, he tells me, almost no instructions from his government.

Mr. Freitas-Valle of Brazil has demonstrated on this Committee the same practical common sense which he showed on the Coordination Committee at San Francisco. . . .

Mr. [Ivan] Kerno who is the Czechoslovak representative has made many useful contributions to the discussions and has shown a surprising independence of the Soviet Union. He found it necessary to vote with the Soviet Union on the question of the rotating chairmanship of the Committee, and once the Soviet Union had shown its bitter dislike of the United Nations Information Organization he had to cease being its champion. But on other matters, and especially in the discussions over the secretariat of the Preparatory Commission, he has taken a line entirely at variance with that taken by the Soviet representative. In the discussion on the secretariat he vigorously opposed the Soviet contention that the senior members should all be members of the national delegations of the fourteen countries represented on the Executive Committee. He further stated that he "viewed with great apprehension" a system under which some of the temporary international secretariat would be paid by national governments and some by the international organization and he went so far as to urge that payments made by governments to their officials who were lent to the secretariat should be refunded to them later by the United Nations organization.

The representatives of Yugoslavia and Chile have contributed almost nothing to the discussions and the temporary representative of Mexico, their Ambassador here, has not said a word. Indeed, the Ambassador is reported to have said that he did not know anything about the subjects to come before the Committee,

that he had not read anything about them and that he would not
say anything, but that he would come to the meetings so that the
Committee would not number thirteen. No doubt when the chief
delegate of Mexico arrives, Senor [Luis] Padilla Nervo, he will
make a useful contribution to the discussions.

Dr. van Roijen, the chief Netherlands' delegate is not as useful a member of the Committee as his alternate, Mr. [M. A.] Pelt. [I
soon became a great admirer of Herman van Roijen. His failure to
impress me during the first two weeks of the committee was because he was new to the work.]

The Iranian representative, Mr. [Nasrullah] Entezam, does
not say much but what he says is almost invariably to the point
and it looks as if he will be a good chairman of the sub-committee
on general questions.

An international secretariat

The attitude taken by the Soviet delegation on the secretariat
of the preparatory commission is a forecast, I am afraid, of the very
considerable difficulties which the Executive Committee and the
Organization will face in matters relating to the [U.N.] Secretariat. It is scarcely an exaggeration to say that the Soviet believe
that all the senior posts in an international civil service should be
held by national civil servants and that only the junior posts
should be held by international civil servants. The national civil
servants would be merely loaned temporarily to the Organization.

You may have noted, for example, Mr. Gromyko's statement
that "the main creative work" of the Executive Committee would
be done by sub-committees composed of representatives of delegations, that experts should not be on the staff of the secretariat and
that "the functions" of the secretariat were strictly technical and
organizational. Moreover, the national officials lent to the secretariat would remain members of their delegations and would be
paid by their national governments. . . .

Relations with the press

The discussions in the Executive Committee on relations
with the press indicate the difficulties which the United Nations
will face in dealing with this problem. The Soviet delegation did
not want to have any of the meetings of the Executive Committee
open to the press, except formally staged meetings at which the

Committee would, without debate, adopt some memorandum on which it had previously reached agreement. Apart from that, they thought the press ought to be content with formal press releases. While it is hard to say how they can even try to prevent the General Assembly from holding most of its meetings in public, it does seem likely that they will do their best to ensure that no real discussion in the Security Council goes on in public, and they may also try to ensure that Assembly committees dealing with political problems should hold their meetings in private.

On the question of the relations of the Executive Committee with the press the United States delegation has taken a line very similar to that taken by the Soviet delegation. Mr. Noel-Baker has taken an extreme position on the other side. In his opinion the meetings of the Executive Committee should always be open to the press unless the Committee is discussing questions of personality. He is convinced that this would not prejudicially affect the frankness of discussion nor otherwise lower the standards of discussion, but would actually improve discussion and that it would help to educate the public.

The Soviet versus the western world

Thus on most of the controversial questions which have so far come before the Committee, the Committee has usually been divided with the Soviet world on one side and the rest of the world on the other. It is possible that this may not be the line-up in discussions over the preparation of the agenda for the first sessions of the Security Council. On this point the United States delegation is taking an extremely restrictive line, and the Soviet delegation has not shown its hand.

7 September 1945. Friday.
9:30 p.m.
I was put on the spot at the Executive Committee meeting today. Stettinius made his first appearance and read a statement calling for us to finish our work by October 15, have a three-week's meeting of the Preparatory Commission followed immediately by a two or three-week's meeting of the first General Assembly which would be a purely organizational meeting. [A full-dress Assembly would be held about the end of April.] I had written Ottawa two weeks ago saying this was likely to come up, and setting forth the

line I thought we should take. About a week ago I wired saying that it was coming up soon and in the absence of instructions I would take this line. I got no reply. Stettinius was followed by Noel-Baker who much to my surprise did not put forward the contrary proposal which he had been supporting hitherto—that the first Assembly should be a bang-up meeting which would discuss questions of substance. Instead he gave general support to Stettinius. So did the Soviet, China, the Netherlands and Brazil. Then I came in with my sole dissenting voice suggesting that the Assembly be postponed till January in order to give time to make the preparations necessary to make it a great town meeting of the world. Afterwards Professor C. K. Webster congratulated me on my speech and said his Minister also was impressed by it. The discussion is now adjourned until Monday afternoon when it resumes at a public meeting held in the Chamber the House of Commons used to meet in at Church House and in the presence of 140 newspapermen. If I don't get instructions to the contrary from Ottawa I'll have to perform on this stage. Certainly I'm being put through the hoops. . . .

The only bright thing I've heard lately is a remark made by a strip-tease artist here from whom an Indian was trying to get back a £10,000 ring he had given her. The magistrate asked her if she knew what unsophisticated meant. She said she wasn't sure but she thought it meant someone who wasn't a prostitute. . . .

7 September 1945.
Statement at the Executive Committee.[7]
The Assembly, in Senator Vandenberg's phrase, is the Town Meeting of the World, and in the state in which the world is today, it is, I think, desirable that that Town Meeting, which will discuss questions of substance, and not purely matters of organization, meet as soon as possible. Therefore, I would suggest that we might think in terms of having the first meeting of the Assembly to discuss questions of substance take place somewhat earlier than April. Another consideration which it would seem that we would have to bear in mind is that, regardless of the views of the majority of the 50 member nations, even if it is a very considerable majority, that the first meeting of the Assembly confine itself to organizational questions, that decision may not meet with the concurrence of a minority. The result would probably be that the General As-

sembly, or certain of its members, would in fact, regardless of the general view, not confine itself to a discussion of purely organizational questions at its first meeting. Now, if that is so, the choice before us is not a choice between a purely organizational meeting of the General Assembly and a meeting which would discuss world problems as well as organizational ones, but between an ill-prepared meeting of the General Assembly and a well-prepared one. If the General Assembly is to secure the respect of public opinion throughout the United Nations, it is of great importance that, as soon as it starts discussing questions of substance, it should demonstrate conclusively its ability to deal with delicate problems of international significance in a wise and useful manner. . . .

I would, therefore, throw out, purely as a suggestion, the following sort of timetable which we might aim at. There should be a meeting of the Preparatory Commission somewhere around October 15 to November 1, which would receive from this Executive Committee the report of the Executive Committee on organizational questions. The Preparatory Commission . . . would go over our work, would not discuss questions of substance, and would be followed by a meeting of the first Assembly toward the middle or end of January. Since the first Assembly would be composed of the same states, or roughly the same states, as compose the Preparatory Commission, it would rubber stamp the decisions of the Preparatory Commission on organizational matters. It would be only a question of two, three days', four days' work, and the General Assembly could then go on to discuss questions of substance. I don't put that forward as a definite proposition, but merely as something which we might consider. It is in a sense a compromise. It postpones Mr. Stettinius' organizational meeting of the General Assembly for two months; it brings forward the Town Meeting of the World three months.

8 September 1945. Saturday.
10:00 a.m.
It's a wet morning. I'm lunching with E. C. Carter today [secretary-general of the Institute of Pacific Relations], with James MacColl tomorrow [Labour M.P., a friend from Oxford days], and dining with the Netherlands member of the Executive Committee and a Netherlands underground leader tomorrow.

10 September 1945.
To the Department of External Affairs.
Mr. Gerig told a story about the choice of Sir Eric Drummond as
the first Secretary-General of the League of Nations. He said that
after the discussions about the League had been going on for some
time in Paris Clemenceau called someone to him and said, "Who
is that official in the corner over there who works so efficiently but
never says anything?" When he was told that it was Eric Drummond, the private secretary to Lord Balfour, he said that Drummond was the obvious man for Secretary-General.

11 September 1945. Tuesday.
10:00 a.m.
Yesterday's meeting went off all right so far as I am aware. I was
able to let Hasluck of Australia and Noel-Baker carry the ball and
come in towards the end with a compromise.

13 September 1945. Wednesday.
11:15 p.m.
I am getting very nice remarks about my two longish speeches
which I gave to the Executive Committee of Stettinius and the
ambassadors [on 7 and 10 September]. Webster of the U.K. delegation and Gerig of the U.S. (who are both the second-in-
commands) said my first was the best speech given during all the
meetings of the Committee. Also the nice Jersey Islander who
translates at two of the committees I talk a lot at said he had never
in eighteen years of translating at international councils and conferences seen a clearer mind in operation and that I was beautifully easy to translate because the argument was so logical. So I
guess I'll be getting a swelled-head. . . . Tomorrow morning
there is to be another Executive Committee meeting open to the
press—the fourth in the series on Stettinius' motion to speed up
the work of the Committee. Instead of speeding it up he has, of
course, jammed the works. All with the best of intentions but he is
too simple for this sort of work. . . . The betting about the
headquarters of the Organization is still 50:50 Geneva vs. San
Francisco. Everything is in favour of Geneva except the Soviet
objections.

16 September 1945.
To the Department of External Affairs.[8]
As soon as I brought forward my formula [on revising the Stettinius resolution along the lines of my statement of 7 September] in the Committee it was supported by Mr. Hasluck of Australia. This aroused Mr. Gromyko's suspicion and he made a statement which Mr. Noel-Baker not unfairly paraphrased later . . . "Some of the members of the Committee who have views I do not like support this compromise and therefore I oppose it." Mr. Noel-Baker proceeded to give Mr. Gromyko a tough lecture on how impossible it would be for any committee to reach a compromise if the Soviet delegation took this line.

17 September 1945. Monday.
11:15 p.m.
To Mother.
We have now moved our office [from Canada House] to 14 Berkeley Street where the Canadian Legation to the Allied governments used to be. . . . The Legation has a floor in a new office building just between Berkeley Square and Piccadilly. One advantage is that only a few yards away is the Berkeley Hotel Buttery where you can get lunch or dinner for five or six shillings.

20 September 1945. Thursday.
10:00 p.m.
Last week when I wrote you I said I was being put through the hoops. The last 36 hours I've been put through the wringer. We have been wasting—because of US and Soviet tactics—a frustratingly large amount of time during the past two weeks. Everybody talked about speeding the work up but all they did was to slow it down and keep on saying that we should cut down the amount of work we were supposed to do. Turgeon was sitting in the Executive Committee for Canada two days ago and I was advising him. He got everything mixed up. [W. F. A. Turgeon, ambassador in Brussels, was chief delegate of Canada to the Executive Committee from 17 September to 27 October 1945. The meeting on 18 September was the first he had attended and it is not surprising that he got everything mixed up.] I finally got him to ask the chairman to let me speak and I gave an impassioned plea against

the Soviet-US proposal that we should revise the terms of reference of the committees which it had taken us two weeks to draw up. It went over quite big.

Yesterday morning I had no committee so dictated a memorandum on how to speed up the work of the committees. I revised it at noon, sold it to Turgeon at 2:15, showed it to the representatives of Iran, Australia, Netherlands, Chile, Mexico, China; got their general support and permission from the Netherlands and Mexico to put the resolution down in their names as well as Canada; did this by 5:30, revised it and gave it to the secretariat for mimeographing in French and English at 6:00; woke up in the morning with some ideas on how to introduce it; jotted down a 200 word speech from 9:30 to 9:40 a.m.; had it typed while I was attending a secretariat committee meeting at 10:15; had it mimeographed by 11:15; sold it to Turgeon when he arrived at the conference at 11:30; persuaded him to let me sit at the conference table instead of him; then the chairman [René] Massigli (the French Ambassador) called on me to introduce the resolution; Gromyko (the Soviet Ambassador) objected to considering the tripartite resolution on two grounds—24 hours notice had not been given and another document had precedence; I said nothing and he won his point; then I got Massigli's eye and after two sentences devoted to the other document launched into my speech and gave it to the press; the acting secretary withdrew the rival document; the tripartite resolution was taken up and in an hour and a quarter adopted (all three pages) with only minor changes. . . .

I am now limiting myself to three committees—Assembly, Secretariat, Security Council. The first two are going very well and I like working on them, especially the one on the Secretariat. The third is terrible due to American stupidity and Soviet malevolence but I think the UK is going to stage a revolution tomorrow and perhaps things will improve. . . .

There's still nothing new on where the seat of the Organization will be. The only two cities mentioned are Geneva and San Francisco. If there is a deadlock over them some compromise place may have to be selected. . . .

Don't worry about me. I am really finding this the most interesting job I've ever done. You know that I'm not happy unless I'm working to the limit on a job I like. So I don't really mind that I've no time for anything but work. It keeps me from getting lonely

until suddenly it hits me hard when I have a moment to myself—
usually when I'm walking through the Green Park. For some reason or other you and the Green Park go together in my mind.

21 September 1945.
To the Department of External Affairs.
[Report on a discussion at a Commonwealth dinner meeting of
where the headquarters of the U.N. should be located.] In my brief
intervention I emphasized the severely practical consideration
that if we were to go anywhere else but Geneva we would have to
camp for the first few critical years of the life of the Organization.

26 September 1945. Wednesday.
10:00 p.m.
The memorandum on the organization of the Preparatory Commission, the heads of which I jotted down when I was in the middle of writing you last Thursday, became a long dictated memorandum on Friday morning and has now been accepted by the
secretariat and Stettinius and will probably be adopted on Friday
at the Executive Committee. So I am becoming a grey eminence.
All in order to be sure that I'm going to get home for Christmas.

3 October 1945. Wednesday.
9:40 p.m.
I had this morning free for writing telegrams to Ottawa and memoranda for committees; then a very pleasant lunch with Ben
Gerig of the U.S. delegation at Bootle's (Club), and a meeting of
the Executive Committee from 2:30 to 7:00 in private to discuss the
seat of the Organization. . . . The vote went 9 to 3 in favour of
the U.S. with Canada and the U.S. abstaining. The negatives were
U.K., France and the Netherlands (i.e. all the unoccupied European countries). Noel-Baker takes a tragic view of the result and is
going to fight the decision tooth and nail. He thinks it may mean
the death knell of the Organization. His speeches and Massigli's
were brilliant and even moving. They had the weight of argument
and oratory but not of votes. The decision may perhaps be difficult to put into effect since the next question is which city in the
U.S. and some of those who voted for the U.S. are strongly opposed to the west coast. . . .
The news today of the failure of the Big Five Conference is

appalling. We are back again at one of the low points in relations between the western world and the Soviet world—the middle of May all over again. The periodicity seems to be every four or five months. Let's buy a farm and grow peaches.

3 October 1945. Wednesday.
10:00 p.m.
To Mother.
Life has been pretty grim lately and my letters have been few. My time-table is:

9:15:	arrive at office
9:15–10:15:	read night's accumulation of documents and dictate hurried telegrams to Ottawa
10:15:	leave for Church House
10:30 a.m.–7:00 p.m.:	committee meetings
7:15–8:30:	back to office to prepare for the next day
8:45:	dinner
10:30–11:00:	bed

I see no one except my colleagues on the committees with whom I occasionally arrange business lunches or dinners. They are very nice but occasionally I'd like fresh faces. On Sundays I usually get to the office at 11:00 a.m. and do only about five hours work.
. . . London is looking very lovely in the early October glow. I walk back from Church House to this office at 7:00 in the dusk through St. James' and the Green Park by the water's edge and it is very beautiful. I have got accustomed to the shabbiness of London now and it doesn't tear my heart any more. But I do wish they would clean up the parks.

12 October 1945. Friday.
3:00 p.m.
I am seizing an opportunity before a meeting of a bloody committee on the Security Council to scribble a note to you since I shall be working until midnight tonight and may not have a chance to write tomorrow morning before the [diplomatic] bag closes.
. . . I think that by working till midnight for the next six days we will finish by next Thursday evening. What the final report will look like to the outsider I don't know. I think that Norman,

Hume, Lou Rasminsky and I could have written the whole thing better in one solid week of work by ourselves. The general world situation is, I am afraid, pretty grim. The world of the atomic bomb presents problems which we seem incompetent to deal with. The new organization of the United Nations can work only if the big three can cooperate and they demonstrate little capacity to cooperate. These are the main terrors but on a lower day-by-day basis there is the depressing thought that if the proceedings of this Committee are any guide the United Nations organization will work at half the speed of the League.

14 October 1945. Sunday.
2:30 p.m.
Our committee meeting is taking place in a horrible din. The workmen are knocking away the brickwork built up outside the windows as protection against bombs. A fine theme for a speech. The protection against the last war being removed while we build up protection against the next. A fine theme and I wish it turns out to be true but our. . . . [I was interrupted.]

16 October 1945.
10:15 a.m.
Yesterday I exploded at the Executive Committee. I enclose *The Times* [16 October 1945] colourless report.

Faulty English in State Documents
Complaint to United Nations Committee.

The use of more simple English in the documents of the Executive Committee of the United Nations Preparatory Commission was urged by the Canadian delegate, Mr. Escott Reid, at yesterday's meeting of the committee in London under the chairmanship of Mr. Noel-Baker, Minister of State. Mr. Escott Reid said that some of the documents were full of crimes against the English language. Great state documents should be written in accordance with the great traditions of the language, in simple, sensible English.

18 October 1945. Thursday.
10:45 a.m.
I am constantly surprised by how well I feel. The hours I keep are

pretty much 9:30 to midnight of intensive work but I seem to have made myself into a machine which can operate at that speed for that number of hours a day. All I am is a machine. I have virtually no private life, no private thoughts and live a completely sub-human and uncivilized life—with no interest in books or plays or friends. The only thing which makes me believe I am something more than a brain is that I still feel more than a craftsman's interest in the work. I still feel that, though what we are doing may not mean much, it may make a little difference—it may however slightly lessen the appallingly large odds in favour of another war. The general outlook is terrifying in the real sense of the word. I am glad I have to work so hard that I have little time to think about it. Sometimes I am glad you are not here because I would scarcely see you anyway. Sometimes I wish to God you were here so that I could have something to hang onto—some hand to hold in the dark. Perhaps I can get some hope back after a week's holiday. Perhaps the tide will turn again as it did in the middle of the San Francisco Conference. Perhaps the present Russian tactics are merely moves in a small game and not preliminary moves in a life-and-death struggle.

19 October 1945.
To the Department of External Affairs.[9]
[Charles E. Bohlen of the State Department was in London for the first meeting of the five-power Council of Foreign Ministers set up at the Potsdam Conference. The meeting was a failure. See letter of 3 October above. We lunched together on 19 October. I reported to Ottawa on Bohlen's views.] It was clear that what the Russians were really interested in was a three-power alliance and not a general international organization. What was more disturbing was that the Soviet Government gave a peculiar interpretation to the doctrine of the necessity of unanimity of the three great Powers. By this they meant that the other two great powers should support the third great power in questions arising in that power's special sphere of interest. This had been demonstrated in messages which the State Department had received from the Soviet Government on the Polish dispute. As one member of the British Embassy [in Washington] put it, it was not a question of "You stop kicking my dog around" but "You let me do what I like with my Poles."

22 October 1945. Monday.
9:00 p.m.
My temporary membership in the Travellers Club has at last come through due to Gilbert Ryle's kindness. [Ryle had been one of my tutors at Oxford in the late twenties.] It is a great convenience. I have dined there Saturday and today. The meals are good—as London goes—, are cheaper than restaurants and are served in a non-restaurant manner. Also you can sit afterwards in a pleasant smoking room. . . . It now looks as if the Committee will go on till Thursday night. Today's meeting was terrible. Turgeon was good enough to suggest I should take his place while the reports of the committees I was on were being discussed so I carried the ball this afternoon and gave what I am told was an eloquent speech. It was a very trying day. Gromyko, the Soviet representative, was more obdurate than usual. The U.S. chairman is going to try to persuade him to a compromise tonight on a small point concerning the Security Council. I pity him his task.

Last night I arranged a dinner for Norman [Robertson] at the private room in the Churchill Club—van Roijen and Pelt of the Netherlands; C. K. Webster and Jebb of the UK; Gerig from the US; and Hasluck from Australia. It went off very well except that the red wine the club supplied at over a pound a bottle was terrible.

On the way to the Churchill Club we stopped at my office to pick up my liquor—gin, whiskey and South African brandy. Coming down from the office we got in the elevator on the third floor. I pushed the button for the ground floor. The elevator went down one foot and then stopped with a really sickening jolt. We pressed all the buttons in the elevator but nothing happened. All this was in complete darkness except for the light from my cigarette lighter which gave out after fifteen minutes. We had with us the army chauffeur of Norman's car. His idea was to use brute force to open the elevator gates. He wrenched and pulled and battered and nothing happened. There was no use yelling because there was nobody in the building and no one from the street could possibly hear us. The chauffeur kept battering. Norman kept pushing buttons. Our guests kept waiting at the Churchill Club. We—without confessing it to each other—gave up all hope and had to contemplate spending fourteen hours in the elevator till someone came in in the morning. We could not even all lie down at the same time. Since we had liquor with us we would probably all have got stone drunk. However after we had been in twenty minutes (it seemed an hour) Norman pushed a button and the elevator went up protestingly to the top floor where we all got out in pitch blackness and thankfully walked downstairs leaving a sign on the elevator downstairs—"Out of order." It was a shattering experience.

24 October, 1945. Wednesday.
9:40 p.m.
The Executive Committee has been meeting today 10:30–1:15, 3:00–4:00 and 8:30 on. It looks as if we shall go on to midnight since we are doing our best to end the Committee tomorrow evening. . . .

I have got the name of a real honest to God farmhouse near Wantage on the Berkshire downs near the Ridge Road which I walked along after my viva [examination in Oxford in 1929.] I wrote to the farmhouse today asking if they could put me up for a week beginning next Monday. I do hope they can manage it. It's so simple a place that I believe I shall be expected to make my own bed and help with the dishes.

I am now sitting back on the newspaper bench [at the Executive Committee] beside Syd Gruson of the *N.Y. Times*. . . . I've just reintroduced myself to Saville Davis [of the *Christian Science Monitor*]. He was transferred here two months ago and his wife (lucky man) is coming over in two weeks time.

It now looks as if the Soviets are not going to blow this conference up. That is one of the few cheerful things that is happening.

27 October 1945. Saturday.
10:15 a.m.
The Committee is dragging on and on. It now looks as if it should finish today or tomorrow. We shall decide today when the Preparatory Commission is to meet. It looks more and more unlikely that the Assembly will meet until after the New Year.

31 October 1945. Wednesday.
6:00 p.m.
As soon as the Executive Committee was finished, 8:30 p.m., Sat-

urday, after a six hour meeting, I went down with a cold. It shows the triumph of mind over matter. As long as I had to keep up I fought the bug off. As soon as I let my defences down he pounced in on me. I think I could have fought it if I'd spent Sunday and Monday in bed but I had promised the Canadian newspapermen a press conference on Monday morning to explain the report of the Executive Committee to them and so had to go to the office on Sunday to make notes for the talk. However I've spent most of yesterday and today in bed. Tomorrow I'll work on some papers at the hotel. Friday I'll see Norman [Robertson] and Saturday at 1:45 p.m. I'm off to my farm in the Berkshires where I may stay ten days or even two weeks and try to get some vitality. At present I feel like an orange that has been sucked dry. . . .

I've bought "The Unquiet Grave" by Palinurus [Cyril Connolly]. . . . It has many good things. . . . "Those of us who were brought up as Christians and who have lost our faith have retained the Christian sense of sin without the saving belief in redemption. This poisons our thought and so paralyzes us in action. . . ." Palinurus has the same worries about being forty that I have. Now that it is three quarters over I feel it has been a watershed. I've grown a lot older—whether it's an improvement or not I don't know. I've grown a lot older for the most part away from you. I think the term for my year is manic depression—long periods of creative excitement, short periods of terrible gloom. My only escape from gloom is to work harder than ever. Perhaps in the next two weeks I can find a substitute drug. And the year cut in two by an event which has made all history ancient except that of the last three months—the use of the atomic bomb.

I have a feeling that one thing which might save us is if history could be made to stand still for six months while people like Norman went away to a monastery to meditate. The problems are too big to be solved by tired minds which are also trying to solve day-by-day problems.

In September I had a talk with I. F. Stone, the American journalist, who was stopping off in London on his way to Palestine. I had known him when I was at the Canadian embassy in Washington and liked and respected him. I urged him to stay in London and not go to Palestine. The big story, I said, was not in Palestine; it was in London. Here in London he would, if he stayed long enough, feel the wartime alliance with the Soviet Union rapidly eroding away under his feet. It seemed to me, for example, that the widespread wartime enthusiasm of the people of Britain for the Soviet Union was turning into contempt and fear. British soldiers brought home stories of the wholesale atrocities of the Soviet armies in occupied territories in Europe and of the way the Soviet authorities treated their own people returning home from prisoner-of-war camps and displaced-persons' camps. The newspapers were full of these stories and of how the Soviet government was imprisoning, torturing, and killing the leaders of the agrarian and social-democratic parties in eastern Europe. My plea to I. F. Stone was unsuccessful; he did not stay in London but went on to Palestine.

While public support in Britain (and presumably in other western countries) for close relations with the Soviet government was dwindling, the relations between western governments and the Soviet government were becoming increasingly strained. My recollection is that in 1944 the western powers did not have high hopes of cooperation with the Soviet Union in dealing with the problems of the postwar world. They did not, however, contemplate that the borderline in Europe between the Soviet troops advancing from the east and western troops advancing through France and Italy would become a borderline between a Soviet empire and the western world. They believed that a buffer zone would be created between the two spheres, consisting of Poland, Czechoslovakia, Hungary, Romania, and Bulgaria. These states would be friendly to the Soviet Union but they would not be dominated by it. As the year 1945 drew to a close it was becoming increasingly clear that the Soviet Union intended to establish puppet regimes in these states.

I had been in London two months when Norman Robertson, the head of the Canadian Department of External Affairs, came to London with the prime minister of Canada. One night after dinner he told me in the strictest confidence that the Canadian government had just learned of the existence of an extensive Soviet spy ring in Canada through the defection of Gouzenko, a cypher clerk at the Soviet embassy. This spy ring had been operating since 1942. Seventeen members of the Soviet embassy in Ottawa were members of it. There was proof that it included a cypher clerk in the Department of External Affairs and it was possible that other members of the Department were in the spy ring. Now, when we take the existence of spy rings as a matter of course, it is hard to realize the shattering effect in October 1945 of learning that at the very time we had been allies in war, the Soviet government had been operating a spy ring in our country whose Canadian members were mainly idealistic supporters of communism. (I did not, of course, in my personal letters or in official correspondence at the time even hint at the Gouzenko affair. It was not until 15 February 1946, about four months later, that it became public.)

The worsening relations between the Soviet Union and its former allies in the autumn of 1945 were reflected in the work of the Executive Committee. As the meetings of the Committee went on I found it difficult not to conclude from Soviet behaviour that the Soviet government was deliberately trying to sabotage efforts to make the U.N. into an efficient and effective organization, for fear that it would be used against the Soviet Union by the United States and that, if these efforts were unsuccessful, it would refuse to ratify the U.N. Charter. More and more often, at the meetings of the Committee and its sub-committees, Gromyko would assert that some proposal which was clearly going to be adopted was a violation of the Charter. An uneasy feeling began to grow within me that he was under orders from Moscow to accumulate a list of so-called violations of the Charter which could be used by the Soviet government as justification for a decision by the Soviet Union not to ratify the Charter. What was also strange and perturbing to me was that Gromyko, though he could count on only three votes out of fourteen (his own and those of Czechoslovakia and Yugoslavia), often gave the impression that he believed he spoke for the majority of mankind.

Whether the Soviet government was in fact in September and October 1945 contemplating not joining the U.N. I do not know. I do know that when Gromyko returned to London from Moscow for the opening of the Preparatory Commission on 24 November he agreed to many proposals he had previously opposed.

Paul Hasluck of Australia had the same sort of apprehension as I had. In his memoirs he writes:

From July to October 1945 there were indications of uncertainty in the Soviet Union's attitude towards the United Nations. I only guess at the possible reasons—a reaction to the change in calculations of power following the launching of the atom bomb, an internal crisis in the Soviet Union itself, preoccupation with the immediate post-war diplomatic task of building security on their western frontier and adjusting boundaries and creating buffers between the Soviet Union and Germany. As it seemed to me in the work of the Executive Committee, the Soviet Union was stalling until about mid-October. At that time their stiffness eased a little and the prospect of their continued membership of the United Nations and active participation in its affairs became clearer.[10]

5

The Preparatory Commission

24 NOVEMBER–23 DECEMBER 1945

2 November 1945.

To the Department of External Affairs.

Draft Memorandum on the Nature of the Instructions which might be given to the Canadian Delegation to the Preparatory Commission.[1]

The Preparatory Commission has an important creative job to do. The San Francisco Conference established in the Charter the foundation of an international organization to maintain peace. The Preparatory Commission has to draw up plans for making this basement habitable. The job can be put in another way. The Charter is similar to a written national constitution. A national constitution must be supplemented by constitutional statutes. The job of the Preparatory Commission is to prepare the constitutional statutes to supplement the constitution. These statutes take the form of rules of procedure for the various organs, staff regulations, financial regulations, and so on. In addition the Preparatory Commission has to prepare the agendas for the first sessions of the principal organs and documentation on the items on these agendas sufficient to form the basis of intelligent discussion. In this aspect of its work it is doing the work that the international secretariat, when once established, will do at subsequent meetings of the organs.

The Preparatory Commission is the Secretary-General in commission. Under the Interim Arrangements Agreement it is instructed to make "provisional arrangements for the first sessions of the General Assembly, the Security Council, and the Economic and Social Council, and the Trusteeship Council, for the establishment of the Secretariat and for the convening of the International Court of Justice. . . . " The Interim Arrangements Agreement makes no distinction between the work which the

Preparatory Commission is required to do for the various organs. Attempts to whittle away the powers and duties of the Preparatory Commission by distinguishing between the Court and the Security Council on the one hand and the other organs on the other hand are a manifest violation of the language and spirit of the Agreement. The Preparatory Commission is a creature of the constitutional conference held at San Francisco. It is not the General Assembly in embryo.

The unhappy experience of past years and especially of the past few months has demonstrated that, if the first meeting of an international deliberative body is to be successful, agreement must be reached in advance on the rules of procedure which are to govern its deliberations. Agreement should also be reached on the agenda and the agenda should be adequately documented. If agreement on rules of procedure and agenda is not reached before the first sessions of the organs of the United Nations there is great danger that the first sessions of these organs will be devoted to long debates on procedural questions. The resulting shock to public confidence will be great and the prestige of the United Nations will be gravely endangered. On the other hand, if the organs of the United Nations can, in a matter of a few days after their establishment, get themselves organized and in a position to get down to their real business, the prestige of the United Nations will be high and the peoples of the world will see a glimmer of hope for the future. . . .

Experience at previous conferences has also demonstrated that the time to take a firm line, and if necessary an extreme position, is at the very beginning of a conference. At the beginning of a conference, but not at the end, it is possible to submit papers with a notation that they are "tentative proposals circulated as a basis of discussion and do not necessarily bind the Canadian delegation." Soviet tactics at international conferences have taught us the value of adopting a fairly extreme position at the opening of a conference since retirement from that position to middle ground can then be played up as being a great concession made in a conciliatory spirit in an effort to secure unanimity. . . .

As far as the Secretariat is concerned the main task of the Canadian delegation will be to resist efforts by the Soviet Union, aided perhaps by some Latin American states, to play down the importance of efficiency, competence and integrity in appointments to the Secretariat and to play up the importance of equitable geographical distribution. The best way of meeting these attempts to undermine the international Secretariat is by appealing to the precise language of the Charter on this point. The Soviet Union, again assisted by some Latin American states including perhaps Mexico, will try to insist that each national government have the right to veto the appointment of any of its nationals to the international Secretariat. They may indeed insist that all applications for employment or offers for employment in the international Secretariat should be channelled through national foreign offices. These suggestions should be resisted. . . .

One question which will arise in many committees is the nature of expert committees of the Organization. The Soviet position is that the way to appoint an expert committee is to appoint, on the basis of equitable geographical distribution, a given number of states as members of the committee and to authorize each state to appoint an expert. The Soviet apparently find it impossible to conceive of an expert committee of persons appointed in their individual capacity and because of their personal competence and taking orders, not from any single state, but acting as experts responsible to the whole Organization. Soviet proposals to constitute expert bodies on a state rather than a personal basis should be resisted.

2 November 1945.
Cable.
Norman Robertson says I will be definitely transferred to Department [of External Affairs] after this assignment and that you would be safe in renting a house in Ottawa. My promotion to Counsellor is going through immediately at salary of 5400. If the Preparatory Commission ratifies the recommendation to hold Assembly in first week in January I shall be unable to get home until after Assembly meeting which will probably last three weeks. My only chance of getting home by the new year is if Assembly is postponed. Am leaving tomorrow fourteen days holiday at Berkshire farm. Much love.

7 November 1945. Wednesday.
9:30 a.m.
Eastmanton Farm.
The next few months and years are going to be crucial for the human race. It looks like "world state or perish." Canada has far

heavier responsibilities and much greater influence in the solution of this problem than her strength warrants—because of her
knowledge of atomic research and her possession of uranium. In
the Department I will—unless something goes wrong—be one of
the top three in discussions of large political questions. So my
guess is that that is where my place in the battle is. This may be the
kind of battle where at a moment in time one will know for a
certainty that the battle is lost and that we must prepare to face
destruction of most of the world and its people, plague, pesti-
lence, famine and social anarchy. There are four things we could
do: go on with the daily round, the common task; prepare one's
soul for God; eat, drink and be merry; try to find some place where
the chances of our children and ourselves surviving the anarchy
would be somewhat greater than as civil servants in a national
capital. Perhaps a mainly self-sufficient farm in Bruce County.

10 November 1945. Saturday.
Eastmanton Farm.
To son, Patrick.
Looking back at the Executive Committee's work, it went off very
well. The worrying thing for the last half of the work—ever since
the Foreign Ministers' meeting failed—was whether the Russians
would stop cooperating in the Executive Committee and find
some reason for withdrawing from its activities. The fact that they
didn't is one of the few encouraging things that have happened in
recent months. . . . The conversations in Washington between
Truman, Attlee and King [on the control of atomic energy] are
about the most important thing that's happened since the atomic
bomb and that was the most important since the birth of Christ.

11 November 1945. Sunday.
7:00 p.m.
Eastmanton Farm.
The country seems to look lovelier every day—the meadows and
the winter wheat are so green, the leaves of the trees so brown, and
the sky so blue. It is hard to believe it is November. . . . The
farmhouse is three hundred years old, I would think. It is heavily
thatched and surrounded by farm buildings. Some of the walls
between rooms are 6 feet thick, made of mud and wood. Yesterday
the hunt which was holding its first meeting for many years gal-

loped past in the manor park only a hundred yards from the farm. . . . Only two or three pink costumes, lots of hounds, and about fifty riders. It was a pretty sight on a sunny day but I was glad the fox got away. Mr. Matthews [the farmer I was staying with] has a good deal of country sense. The lord of the manor has no money. Mr. Matthews wishes some new-rich person would buy the manor and the farms since they would be able to throw some money around in the village, support the local charities, etc. In return he would think it only fair to be deferential to him and treat him as a gentleman. From my reading of Trevelyan's [social] history [of England] this is the way the yeoman and the tenant farmer have behaved for six hundred years.

13 November 1945. Tuesday.
5:30 p.m.
Eastmanton Farm.
To Mother.
Norman Robertson and I drove out to the country three Sundays ago to see some friends of his. He is obsessed with the problems of the atomic bomb. He is afraid that one day they will start going off and that the statesmen of the world will say, in surprise, like the clumsy maid, "It just came to pieces in my hands." We were talking about how individuals found a private refuge from the nightmares of the future. I said I thought it was hardest on people of the generation of Dad and yourself because you had been brought up in a decent and humane world which believed that things were getting better and would continue to get better—and that you had taken refuge in a profound scepticism about things temporal.

15 November 1945. Thursday.
5:45 p.m.
Eastmanton Farm.
I cannot remember how much of the Palinurus quotation on fanaticism and serenity I gave you. He had been talking about people who by going mad find happiness for the first time in their lives.

> When the present slaughter terminates humanity can survive only through a return to the idea of happiness as the highest good, happiness which lies not in power or in the exercise of

the will but in the flowering of the spirit. . . . Somehow, then and without going mad, we must learn from these madmen to reconcile fanaticism with serenity. Each one, taken alone, is disastrous, yet except through the integration of these two opposites there is no great art and no profound happiness—and what else is worth having? For nothing can be accomplished without fanaticism, and without serenity nothing can be enjoyed.

The key phrase—which is I think true—even if one does not accept all the rest is—"Each one, taken alone, is disastrous." I hope you can find serenity from the good earth and help me find it but I fear that a serenity founded only on the good earth will be short-lived and disastrous. The sense of sin and guilt in being happy in a tortured world while doing nothing to stop the torture would soon destroy the happiness. It would be like some good German finding serenity from the good earth on a farm just outside Belsen or Dachau from 1933 to 1945. Much of Europe is now one vast concentration camp and we all live on the edges of it. I wonder also how long the serenity lasted of the serene good-earth Saxon near Breslau who may, during the past six months, have seen all his menfolk between 18 and 50 driven off to Russia, his women-folk between 12 and 60 raped repeatedly week after week, and finally the children, women and old people driven off without possessions to the West. I wonder if today he would not be more likely to be sane, if not serene, if he had fanatically fought against satanism for the past twelve years. So if I try to learn serenity from you I hope you will try to learn fanaticism from me. Your fanaticism need not be the same as mine but if you embrace some fanaticism you will be able to understand mine better.

19 November 1945. Monday.
6:15 p.m.
London (Dorchester Hotel).
The advent of the Labour government has been very flat hitherto but it is picking up a bit today with Morrison's statement on nationalization. But there is none of what I thought there would be of excitement like the early New Deal days in Washington. But they seem to know what they are doing because they increase their majorities in by-elections and municipal elections. The best news of the day is that one of the nicest people—and most intelligent—

I've ever met has arrived to join the Australian delegation—Ken Bailey. He and Wilfred Jenks are coming to have dinner with me tonight. [Jenks, legal adviser to the International Labour Office.]

21 November 1945. Wednesday.
11:50 p.m.
Dana arrived last night about ten o'clock after stops in Minsk and Berlin and circling for hours over England looking for an airport. Today and yesterday London and most of England were covered by dense fog. [Dana Wilgress, ambassador to the Soviet Union, head of the Canadian delegation to the Preparatory Commission.] Things have been very rushed but very pleasant since Dana got here. He really is a nice person. . . .

I am afraid a philosophy of "as if" only provides a consolation when I'm not very tired. When I'm tired it's too great a strain to go in for what seems make-believe or whistling in the dark to keep one's courage up. When I get your support again and the children's I may be less gloomy but for the moment I'm not going on "as if" but the "daily round, the common task."

Escott Reid and Dana Wilgress at the Preparatory Commission, London, on November 26, 1945. Behind, right to left, sit L.-P. Picard and Stanley Knowles.

24 November 1945. Saturday.
9:00 a.m.
I am all dressed up in my short black coat and striped pants for the opening plenary session at 10:00. The Canadian delegates have just arrived at the hotel. I haven't seen them yet. They are bathing and breakfasting. I had hoped to write you a decent letter last night after Noel-Baker's dinner which he gave to the Commonwealth groups but we had a long discussion at the dinner and I didn't get home (?) till nearly midnight. . . .

The two secretaries [of the delegation], [Leo] Malania and Tom Carter, are towers of strength. Dana [Wilgress] is marvellous to work with. Terry [T. W. L. MacDermot of the Department of External Affairs] is attached to the delegation for two weeks, so I think all will go relatively smoothly.

I am starting to read the "Yogi and the Commissar" by Koestler. It is a deeply disturbing book which Norman thinks highly of. Oh hell.

The British—Eden and Bevin—are being very sensible about the necessity of something close to world federation. It may do some good.

27 November 1945. Tuesday.
12:40 a.m.
As you can judge from the hour life is not getting much easier for the time being. I have been hoping from hour to hour to write you a decent letter. Saturday I sat in Executive Committee from 11:00 a.m. to 2:00 a.m. Sunday [the final meeting of the Executive Committee]. At 12:45 a.m. Sunday when we were rapidly getting nowhere I suggested that the U.S. representative and Gromyko be locked in a room together for 15 or 30 minutes so that they could come to an agreement while the rest of us went to the bar and had a drink. The result was that the U.K. representative and I were added to the sub-committee I had proposed and in 45 minutes we did reach agreement.

Sunday morning we spent in delegation meeting. Lunch with Dana [Wilgress] and a very pleasant walk in Hyde Park and Kensington Gardens with Dana and Wynne [Plumptre of the Department of External Affairs] where we saw the Peter Pan statue and the Round Pond. Two more hours of delegation meeting. Dinner with Dana and two Manitoba M.P.s. Then to bed. Today delegation meeting 9:00 a.m., Commonwealth meeting at the F.O., 10:00 a.m.; plenary session 11:00 a.m.; office in the early afternoon; steering committee 5:00 p.m.; informal inner steering committee 6:00 p.m.; meeting with advisers in my room over a bottle of whisky 9:00–12:30. It is fun. We have a really good delegation— both M.P.s and advisers. I think things are going off well. By Thursday we ought to get into a routine and things may be easier for two weeks or so until the pressure to end gets great.

29 November 1945. Thursday.
12:15 a.m.
I am afraid you will be divorcing me because every letter for a week or more has been a scrappy note preceded by an apology. Life is still grim. Today's schedule was:

9:00–10:00 a.m.	Delegation meeting
10:30–1:00	Committee meeting
1:00–3:00	Lunch with U.S. adviser
3:00–4:45	Office drafting telegrams to Ottawa
5:00–7:15	Committee
7:30–8:00	Massey cocktail party
8:00–9:15	Dinner with delegation
9:30–12:15	Delegation meeting

Last night Dana [Wilgress] phoned Norman [Robertson] for instructions on the headquarters of the Organization and today we got lengthy instructions so that we are not now operating in a complete fog. The instructions are mine up to 7 out of 10 points; 2 negatives to mine and 1 in between. A fairly good score.

I wish you were here to meet some of the friends I am making. The world has some good people in it.

4 December 1945. Tuesday.
2:15 a.m.
This life is madness. We have to have all our amendments in by Wednesday. My Sunday was 8:45 a.m. till 12:30 midnight with short breaks for lunch and tea. Today started at the same time and ended a few minutes ago. We are doing a real job. It's probably the best Canadian delegation ever but it's a matter of nursing, guiding, humouring. The experts are wonderful and Wynne [Plumptre] is a joy.

5 December 1945. Wednesday.
10:15 p.m.
The peak of the work is, I think over or rather we are about to slide
fast down into a valley between two peaks. Terry MacDermot has
just read to me the last memorandum we are sending in before the
deadline at midnight. We must in all have sent in about three
times as much constructive stuff as any other delegation. . . . I
am beginning to feel more at ease at my daily press conferences
and am beginning quite to enjoy them. We have the daily delegation meeting in Dana's sitting room at 9:00. It usually runs on till
10:15 but I leave at 10:00 for my room next door which by then has
been fixed up so that the bed looks like a couch and take my conference which lasts till 10:45 or so. This morning it went on till
11:00. I had Joan Twelvetrees of British United Press, Ross Munro
of the Canadian Press, Burt Richardson, Charlie Nichols (South-
ams), Gerry Clark (Montreal Star). Sometimes I get Cranfield of
the Toronto Telegram. I try to help them understand what is
happening in the eight committees.

Gordon Graydon tells me that in his last weekly article for the
Peel County papers he referred to me as one of Canada's ace diplomats. He considers me as a home-boy in view of Applefield [my
father's summer cottage which was in Peel County]. He's a
good—very good—member of the delegation. The big surprise is
[L.-P.] Picard, the French [Liberal] M.P., who is the best of the
whole lot and is first class. He can take a brief brief which I give
him which touches on delicate ground and turn it into a polished,
urbane speech which makes all the delicate points by indirection
but forcibly. The young French-Canadian from the legal division
of External, Ernest Coté, is also first rate. We are hoping that both
will stay on for the Assembly. We've urged Ottawa by wire to
make the appointments right away.

As the last straw I got today a request from the administrative
section [in the Department of External Affairs] asking me for my
attendance reports for August, September, October and November. I'm going to bracket all the days in the month and put in
one big "On duty." . . .

I've just been interrupted by Gordon Graydon dropping in to
see me about some of the problems on his Economic and Social
Committee. He has a very shrewd flair for tactics in a conference
and is not suspected of it because of his bluffness. I am becoming a

convert to good parliamentarians as our delegates to international conferences provided we have a Wilgress-Reid team to make them work and bring out their talents.

At the meetings of the Executive Committee and the Preparatory Commission the United States and the Soviet Union won a hard-fought bitter battle against Britain, France, and the other western European countries to have the headquarters of the U.N. located in the eastern part of the United States. The first engagement in this battle was on whether the headquarters should be in the United States or in Europe. The United States and the Soviet Union won this engagement with the help of such countries as Australia, Brazil, Chile, and China. Those nations wanted San Francisco as the headquarters and would probably not have voted to locate the headquarters in the United States if they had realized that a decision in favour of the United States would mean not San Francisco, but somewhere in the eastern part of the United States.[2] Rather than that they would probably have preferred a site in Europe. Having secured a decision in favour of the United States with the help of such countries, the United States and the Soviet Union put through a resolution in the second engagement of the battle that the headquarters should be in the eastern part of the United States.

Presumably in the archives of the Soviet government there are memoranda written in 1945 on the problem of where the headquarters of the U.N. should be located. In the absence of such memoranda we can only speculate why the Soviet government campaigned so vigorously for establishing the headquarters in the United States. When Dana Wilgress, then Canadian ambassador to the Soviet Union, learned of the Soviet vote in the Executive Committee in favour of the United States he stated in a despatch to Ottawa on 6 November 1945 that he thought the explanation might be that the Soviet government knew that, if the headquarters were in the United States, the secretary-general of the U.N. could not be an American citizen and the Soviet government might be able to get a Soviet citizen appointed as secretary-general.[3] I agree with the first part of his statement but not with the second. After the other permanent members of the Security Council had at San Francisco rejected the Soviet proposal that each of them would over a ten-year period hold the secretary-generalship for two years, the Soviet government could scarcely have hoped to get a Soviet citizen appointed as secretary-general. What it could reasonably hope for was to deny the post to the United States and one way of making it easier to block the appointment of an American citizen was to have the U.N. headquarters established in the United States. It is significant that it was on 4 June, shortly after the Soviet proposal for a rotating secretary-generalship was turned down, that Gromyko informed Stettinius that the Soviet Union was in favour of the U.N. headquarters being established in the United States.[4] In the event the decision of the Preparatory Commission to establish the headquarters in the United States was used by the Soviet government not only to block the appointment of an American but also of the two Canadians the United States had proposed for the secretary-generalship, Norman Robertson and L. B. Pearson.[5]

It seems to me that the other considerations which the Soviet government took into account in opposing Europe as the headquarters were that it did not want Geneva as the headquarters since the Soviet Union had been expelled from the League in Geneva and this rankled, and it did not want a site in Europe near the borderline between East and West because this would open a window on Soviet efforts to force the countries of Eastern Europe to become *de facto* members of the Soviet empire—a consideration which J. D. Hickerson of the State Department alluded to in his secret memorandum of August 1945, which is quoted below.

In the Preparatory Commission opinion was almost equally divided between supporters of Europe and supporters of the United States. The advocates of Europe therefore wanted the first vote to be on a resolution in favour of the United States since they knew it would not secure a two-thirds majority and would therefore be defeated. Similarly the advocates of the United States wanted the first vote to be on a resolution in favour of Europe since they knew it would be defeated because it, too, would not secure a two-thirds vote. The chairman of the committee decided that the first vote should be on a resolution in favour of Europe.

The Soviet Union put pressure on the countries of Eastern Europe to vote in favour of locating the headquarters in the United States. The United States delegation protested almost up to the end of the debate that it was neutral in the choice between Europe and the United States, but in order to get its way it "worked on" the delegations of friendly countries to "try to line up" the necessary votes, to use terms current at that time in United States delegations to international conferences. Two days before the final vote the United States dropped its pretence of neutrality. On 13 December it informed the Preparatory Commission that on 11 December the Senate and the House of Representatives had by unanimous vote invited the United Nations to establish its headquarters in the United States. The message was clear since the Congress would not have done this unless the administration wanted it—and wanted it badly. The advocates of Europe were now put in the position of turning down a formal invitation from the president and the Congress.

It was because of the pressure from Moscow and Washington that countries such as Canada, which favoured Europe, proposed that voting on the headquarters in the Preparatory Commission be by secret ballot. This proposal was defeated, 24 voting for it and 26 against. The committee then voted on a resolution in favour of Europe; 23 voted for Europe, 25 against, and 2 abstained. In the subsequent vote in favour of the headquarters being in the United States, 30 voted for the United States, 14 against, and 6 abstained. The resolution had secured the necessary two-thirds majority of the votes cast.

I believe that if the voting had been by secret ballot the resolution might have failed to secure a two-thirds majority. Certainly Jan Masaryk of Czechoslovakia, who voted for the United States on the open ballot, would have voted against the United States on a secret ballot. In the open ballot Ethiopia, New Zealand, and Syria abstained, though in the immediately preceding ballot they had voted for Europe. In the early years of the U.N. an abstention by a country friendly to the United States on a resolution which the United States was strongly supporting usually meant that the abstainer was opposed to the resolution but did not wish to carry its opposition to the point of openly voting against the United States. These three countries might therefore in a secret ballot have voted against locating the headquarters in the United States. Thus, even if the United States had in a secret ballot voted for itself rather than abstaining, the vote on the resolution, if by secret ballot, might have been 30 to 18 with 2 abstentions instead of 30 to 14 with 6 abstentions. The resolution would have been defeated.

There is thus a possibility that voting by secret ballot would have resulted in deadlock with neither the supporters of Europe nor the supporters of the United States being able to rally two-thirds of the votes. Out of the negotiations which would have followed the deadlock the result might have been the highly desirable one of the establishment of the permanent headquarters near the borderline in Europe between East and West, possibly Vienna or Copenhagen, and the use of Geneva as temporary headquarters pending the construction of the necessary facilities at the permanent site.

The best presentation of the arguments against stationing the headquarters in the United States was made by Hickerson in a secret memorandum of 22 August 1945 to the secretary of state. Hickerson at that time was deputy-director of the office of European affairs in the State Department. A few years later he was one of the principal authors of the North Atlantic Treaty. He was one of the wisest United States foreign service officers of his generation. The director of the office of European affairs, H. Freeman Matthews, concurred in Hickerson's memorandum. The reasons Hickerson advanced for preferring Europe to the United States were:

(1) The headquarters should be in the territory of a state other than one of the "Big Five," otherwise the state in which it was located would be suspected of exercising too much control over the organization; (2) location in the United States would tend to give the impression that the United Nations Organization was "an American affair"; (3) Europe has been traditionally the trouble center and headquarters should be near the trouble zone; (4) if located in the United States there will be a tendency in this country to say: "Oh yes, Stalin agreed to give the United States its world organization but took care to see to it that it was moved to an ivory tower in the United States far from the scene of the strife where it would not interfere in any way with his writing his own ticket in Eastern Europe"; (5) the location in the United States would tend to promote a European regional organization; and (6) the interest of the American people is sufficiently strong for our Government to give its full support to the organization irrespective of where the headquarters may be located.[6]

There was another argument for Europe, or rather for Geneva, at least as temporary headquarters, which I put at a dinner meeting of the Commonwealth representatives on the Executive Committee held on 21 September. I pointed out that if we went anywhere but Geneva we would have to camp for the first few critical years of the Organization. On 27 March 1946, Charles Ritchie of the Canadian Department of External Affairs reported from New York on what this camping was like. He wrote:

> Conditions in New York make the work of the organization as difficult as possible. The Secretariat have offices scattered all over the place. It is very difficult to get in touch with them and they seem to have difficulty in getting in touch with each other. The members of the Security Council have small, harried, over-worked groups of advisors. Members of each delegation are split in various hotels and spend most of their time when they are not at the Security Council in getting to and from the Bronx.[7]

Paul Hasluck, the Australian representative on the Security Council in its early months in New York, has written:

> One day—and admittedly it was a bad day—I calculated that in an absence from home of about sixteen hours I had spent six hours being rushed here and there in vehicles, about two hours waiting for colleagues who were also trying to rush here and there in vehicles but had been caught in traffic jams, and about another hour either telephoning or waiting the results of other peoples' telephoning—and all for the sake of spending a few hours reading documents and exchanging opinions on matters which gained nothing from being considered in the biggest city in the world.[8]

I knew when I left Ottawa for London at the beginning of August 1945 that, as Hume Wrong put it in a letter to me on 30 August, the general feeling of officials in the Department was that Geneva was "probably the most suitable place, if agreement can be secured on it." By the time the first debate took place in the Executive Committee on 3 October the officials in the Department had not been able to secure a decision from the government and Ottawa had to instruct us to be noncommittal on the headquarters. By 27 November the government was, we were told, inclining to the view that the headquarters should be in Europe but it was not until 6 December that the government was able to make up its mind. It then decided that its first choice was Europe and its second the United States, preferably in the northeastern area. This decision enabled Dana Wilgress, the head of the Canadian delegation to the Preparatory Commission, to become one of the leaders in the Preparatory Commission in the struggle for Europe.

I reported to Ottawa at the conclusion of the Preparatory Commission that the decision to locate the U.N. headquarters in the United States would undoubtedly leave a great deal of bitterness.

> One fortunate thing, however, is that before the United States was chosen it became clear that regardless of what the United States said officially it was pushing very hard to get the seat in the United States. Thus the United States is itself in large part responsible for the choice of the United States as the site, and being in large part responsible it must assume an even greater degree of responsibility than before for the success of the United Nations.[9]

The decision of the United States administration to try to get the headquarters located in the United States was made by President Truman, James F. Byrnes, then secretary of state, and Stettinius against the advice of senior officials in the State Department.[10] The decision of Australia to support a site in the United States was made by H. V. Evatt the Australian foreign minister. Paul Hasluck, the head of the Australian delegation to the Executive Committee, was opposed to the decision. Perhaps later the two governments may have come to the conclusion that the officials were right and they were wrong. A few years after the decision was made Dean Acheson, then secretary of state, wished that the headquarters had been established anywhere except the United States.[11] Paul Hasluck, who became minister for external affairs of Australia and later governor-general, wrote in his memoirs, published in 1980,

> The choice of New York as the headquarters of the United Nations had a very marked and harmful effect on the functioning of the Organization. . . . In my view the United Nations got the wrong sort of establishment as well as one that was inconvenient and costly both for the Organization and the national delegations. An ivory tower, an aseptic hospital

ward or a zoo in a park would be the wrong setting for an international organization but nevertheless the United Nations did need some measures of separateness from the pressures of a striving city and some degree of self-containment. It needed some measure of quietness, calmness and immunity from a wholly national environment. It needed to be lifted out of the sort of commercial, political and social turmoil of such a place as Manhattan. Its fate has been to be submerged in this unhealthy swarming urban swamp and to be washed over by all the strange distortions of publicity, notoriety and sectional greed and prejudice that perpetually move from moon to moon in such a city.[12]

In the fifties President Eisenhower twice warned Canadian prime ministers that if the communist government of China were seated in the U.N. the United Nations would leave the United States and the United States would leave the United Nations. I have always considered that the second part of the warning was a bluff. I said in a despatch to Ottawa in July 1954 that "I have myself too much respect for the intelligence of the American people to believe that they would be prepared to set in motion a series of events which might end by the Soviet bloc and the 'peace area' powers getting control of the name, the goodwill and the assets of the United Nations." I therefore regret that the United States bluff was not called in the fifties, since it might have led to the happy result of the United Nations leaving the United States while the United States remained in the United Nations.

7 December 1945. Friday.
11:50 p.m.
I got back early tonight and intended to write you a chatty letter. I undressed and got to bed to read over some newspaper clippings first. About two hours ago Graydon and Picard came in, followed by Malania, Wilgress, Rive and MacDermot and I've just succeeded in getting them out after a difficult debate about Dana's speech today announcing that Canada supported Europe as the site of the Organization. [Alfred Rive, counsellor at the Canadian High Commission, London.] I'm going to get half a dozen "Do not disturb" signs and put them on all my doors. . . . I'm afraid I have no time for more now. I'm sleepy and bad tempered at being kept from bed by the delegates.

10 December 1945. Monday.
5:30 p.m.
Since I doubt whether I'll have time to write this evening I'm writing now during the translations at the committee meeting on the choice of a headquarters for the United Nations. . . . I stopped writing to listen to Victor Hoo's speech. [Hoo, deputy delegate of China.] It was the best—indeed the only good—speech so far given in favour of the U.S. as the site of the Organization. The bitterness of the thirties came out when he talked of the Europeans being less internationally minded than the Americans. He put his finger on a vulnerable point for many of the most intelligent Europeans—like Noel-Baker and Massigli—are really often more parochial than corresponding Americans.

One accomplishment at the London meetings which gave me particular pleasure was to lead a crusade for the use of simple, direct, forceful language in U.N. documents. This meant that it was necessary to revise most texts in English taken over from League of Nations documents, since these documents were often bad translations from French, and that it was also necessary to rewrite most documents submitted by the United States delegation. Above all it meant discarding the traditional form of resolutions passed by the Council or Assembly of the League, since these were written in a quasi-legal terminology remote from the language normally written by educated people whether in the United States, Britain, the Soviet Union, France, or China. The preamble in the new form would be a direct statement in sentence form without "considerings" and "notings," etc. It would be linked to the operative part of the resolution by "Therefore." The operative part would consist of a series of numbered paragraphs. There would be no subparagraphs. An example of a complicated resolution in the new form is the one on the League of Nations adopted at the first session of the U.N. General Assembly. Partly as a result of my influence the North Atlantic Treaty is in the new form with a few minor exceptions.
    I would not have won the battle for good English if I had not had the support of the most distinguished Australian lawyer who was chairman of the drafting committee of the Preparatory Commission, Kenneth Bailey. He would have been an ornament to the International Court of Justice but he was defeated in the

first election to the Court. Later, when there was a good chance of an Australian being elected, Australia instead put forward the name of a politician who was, in the words Lord Curzon used of Stanley Baldwin, "a man of the utmost insignificance." Our success won us a public accolade from that defender of the English language, A. P. Herbert. But our triumph was short-lived. The first part of the first session of the General Assembly passed some resolutions in the new form, because these resolutions had been put in that form by the drafting committee of the Preparatory Commission. But from then on the organs of the U.N. relapsed into error.

12 December 1945. Wednesday.
11:45 p.m.
The most amusing incident of the conference for me is the hour and a quarter I spent with A. P. Herbert at the Savage Club this afternoon from 6:15 to 7:30. I felt I needed some help in removing jargon from the Charter so I phoned him at the House of Commons and asked him to phone me back. This morning I got in touch with him, explained who I was (and he immediately said—"Oh, you're the man who made the grand attack on jargon a couple of months ago"), and he invited me to meet him at Savages. I went to the meeting armed with the Executive Committee's report, with two appallingly gobbledegookish resolutions which the drafting committee received a few days ago and with a memorandum on them and a revision I'd hurriedly prepared. I showed him the longer of the two resolutions and he read it very gravely. Then I showed him my revision and he became almost lyrical. He kept introducing me to his friends as a knight-errant who had come out of the west to fight what had been considered as a lost battle against jargon. Now he wants to splash me in Punch and on the front page of every newspaper and has already contracted to write an article in the magazine "Truth." I have however his promise to hold everything until the time is ripe so that if the drafting committee accepts my proposals they will share in the glory. . . . A. P. Herbert says that the enclosed [memorandum] which I wrote in about twenty minutes is an historic document. [A. P. Herbert's article appeared in the *Sunday Times* (London) for 23 December 1945 under the title "Battle of Bunkum." See pp. 124–25 below.]

11 December 1945.
Memorandum to the Drafting Committee of the Preparatory
Commission. . . . The second document (a Report from Committee 7) requires careful consideration by the Drafting Committee. The Drafting Committee has been instructed to put this document into final shape and to edit it. The way in which the
Drafting Committee deals with this document will constitute a
precedent for dealing with the reports of other technical committees. The document is also of special importance because it contains the text of a resolution which it is recommended that the
General Assembly should adopt. This resolution may therefore
constitute a model for all future resolutions of the General Assembly of the United Nations.

The resolution is couched in the standard League form: Considering . . . ; and Having been informed . . . ; Reserves . . . ;
Records . . . ; and Declares . . . ; Considering . . . ; Considering . . . ; The General Assembly is willing . . . ; Considering . . .; Considering, however; the General Assembly of the
United Nations decides. . . .

The new organization of the United Nations is making a
fresh start. It would be most valuable if that fresh start were reflected in the form and language of the resolutions which it
adopts, if the United Nations were to make a clean break with
Geneva jargon and League lingo and write its resolutions as
simply and directly as possible. The issue raised is more important than one of stylistic preferences or prejudices. Our confident
hope is that the United Nations is going to be a forceful, decisive
body, not a body in which the emphasis is on 'considerings,' 'notings,' 'reservings,' 'recordings,' but which uses, when necessary,
the srong language of the Charter, 'decide,' 'determine,' 'call
upon,' 'take action.'

The language used in the ordinary resolutions of the General
Assembly or the Security Council may not matter very much. But
the language used in the formal records of important decisions
does matter. Suppose the Security Council decided to take military enforcement measures under Article 42. Is it to do so in a
resolution starting with 'considering' and going on to 'noting,'
'realizing,' 'taking into account,' 'believing' and 'agreeing'? Or is
it to embody its grave decision in simple, crisp, forceful language
appropriate to the gravity of that decision—the kind of language

in which Mr. Churchill announced the decision of the British Government after Dunkirk, in which Marshal Stalin announced the Soviet Union's reply to the German attack in June 1941 or in which Mr. Roosevelt asked Congress to declare a state of war after Pearl Harbour?

A resolution of the Security Council invoking Article 42 should clearly not start with the old-fashioned, flabby League preamble of considerings and notings. The emphasis should be on action. But if we establish in January, 1946, a bad precedent for United Nations resolutions, that precedent will be hard to break when the necessity arises. Therefore it is essential that the Drafting Committee of the Preparatory Commission should, in editing the first draft resolution of an organ of the United Nations to come before it, set a high standard. . . .

14 December 1945. Saturday.
12:30 a.m.
Just a scribble because I am very tired and must go to bed. I think Bailey and I have met with success in persuading the drafting committee to adopt something closer to vernacular English in its draft resolutions for the Assembly. I am keeping my fingers crossed till it gets in type. It's not just my love of English. It's that the United Nations will be a little less remote from the thoughts and feelings of the people if it can write in a language they can understand. The drafting committee goes into continuous session tomorrow or Sunday for a week. It is going to be grim but it's a good committee apart from one Chinese.

17 December 1945.
10:00 p.m.
I think we have won a complete victory over stilted language in United Nations resolutions. Our revised text went back to the committee concerned today and went through without any difficulty. Indeed we were encouraged to carry our good work further. . . . Sydney Gruson of the *N.Y. Times* suggested the other day that my obituary should be—"He died for English." I'm also staving off the corruption of French, Russian, Chinese and Spanish. The Chinese translations of our resolutions in their present form will sound like Chinese. The translations of the old-type resolu-

tions always sounded like translations. Or so my Chinese colleague tells me.

20 December 1945. Thursday.
12:45 a.m.
What is now being called the Bailey-Reid revolution in drafting
international documents has gone through without an open
murmur of dissent, and the more people look at it the more they
like it. The struggle has been fun.

22 December 1945. Saturday.
10:40 a.m.
By tomorrow morning—probably about 4:00 a.m.—all ought to
be over but the shouting—i.e. the plenary meetings. . . . I am
tired but happy. The work of the last five months has been worth-
while. It has been really creative and encouraging. If we can only
keep on building the international order at the rate of the last five
months we may be able to depart in peace from this world. It is
years too early to say a Nunc Dimittis but I can now hope that
someday I can. If the Moscow talks go as well as the Preparatory
Commission we may be able to start the New Year—not with a
clean page—but at least with a page that is not too soiled with the
mistakes of the past.

24 December 1945. Monday.
3:50 p.m.
Brian [Meredith, a first cousin], is calling for me in ten minutes to
take me out to his place at Beaconsfield. . . . My friends tell me
that I am looking older but also people congratulated me on being the only person who seemed to enjoy the Preparatory Commission. I don't think you'll find me changed. If I am I hope it is
for the better. I think I'm more sure of myself, more at peace with
myself because I've been able to create—even if the final product is
anonymous. I am more hopeful of the future because one experiment in the possibility of two worlds working together has succeeded even though most of the other experiments taking place at
the same time have failed. So far as the United Nations is concerned we have only reached the end of the beginning but at least
we have got there without mishap. . . .
    I got three invitations for Christmas dinner—Brian, A. P.

Herbert and [Adrian] Pelt. A. P. Herbert is enjoyable as long as you keep him off politics where he is a terrible reactionary. I like him and he seems to like me.

28 December 1945.
9:00 p.m.
I came back [from Beaconsfield] by a ten o'clock train on Wednesday morning [26 December] and Henry IV with the Grusons was marvellous. [Sydney and Flora Lewis Gruson had invited me to see Lawrence Olivier in *Henry IV*.] . . . Tomorrow I get out of this hotel for eight days. . . . As soon as I get relaxed my accumulated fatigue comes up and hits me and all I want to do is sleep.

28 December 1945.
To N. A. Robertson.
Personal.
You may be amused at the results of the Bailey-Reid struggle to simplify the language of United Nations documents. I therefore enclose A. P. Herbert's article in the *Sunday Times* of December 23rd and a copy of the two documents to which he refers. I hope that we will have your blessing in pressing on with this fight during the Assembly in January. I think we shall have everyone on our side except the legal division of the Foreign Office and perhaps some of the Americans who will be hurt by their jargon being turned into English. . . .

Experience at San Francisco and in London demonstrates that we are the only delegation that is interested in getting good French and English texts which correspond with each other. All the French are interested in is getting a good French text and if, in preparing this text, it becomes obvious that certain improvements should be made in the English text, they have no interest in bringing this to the attention of those who are drafting the English text. . . .

The French delegations at international conferences are so tragically weak that Canada has an opportunity of becoming the leader of the French-speaking countries so far as drafting is concerned. If we adopt this role and are successful in it, we shall increase our chance of getting support from the Latin countries generally in elections to the various Councils.

Article by Sir A. P. Herbert, M.P., in the *Sunday Times* (London) for 23 December 1945.

The Battle of Bunkum

Salute the Drafting Committee of the Preparatory Commission of the United Nations!

Hail and congratulate the Preparatory Commission of the United Nations!

And fire special salvoes from loud and numerous guns in honour of Mr. Escott Reid, of Canada, one of the two representatives of the English language on the Drafting Committee already mentioned. The other member is Professor K. H. Bailey, of Australia, who will not be left out of the story.

It is a great story—Canada and Australia starting, fighting and winning the battle of language in the forum of the world—a battle not for the English language only but for simple language on the cosmic scene.

Many of us, for very many years, have been moaning or moving against official jargon—the language of the law-makers and the law-distributors—against Jungle English. That great master of language, Mr. Churchill, turned his guns, now and then from Hitler to Whitehall. But even his formidable artillery has made no noticeable breach. In the House of Commons, from time to time, a few bold but desperate voices are raised against the letters of the law. In the last Parliament, I remember, in the doodle-time, when we were deliberating reluctantly, in Church House, I raised a row, in vain, about the expression "as soon as may be." I was laughed away. The minister did not know what it meant, but he said it was good enough. In this Parliament the other day, Mr. Reginald Manningham-Buller successfully moved to leave out "as soon as may be" and insert "immediately." Well done.

Such victories are satisfying but few. Amendments about "mere words" are tiresome to the Whips, who want their Bill, and maddening to the Members, who want their beds. They may even be classed as "frivolous," or not be called at all. . . .

How much more difficult and dangerous, then, to make the attempt in an assembly not merely democratic but international, where there are five languages at work, not one! Yet that is what the Preparatory Commission of the United Nations (in which are five "official language groups," Chinese, English, French, Russian and Spanish) has successfully dared and done.

The first shot in this fine campaign was a memorandum submitted by Mr. Escott Reid of Canada to the Drafting Committee on December 11, from which, without apology to anyone, I quote the following wise and revolutionary words: [Then followed the memorandum printed above, pp. 120–21.] I have been privileged to see both the original and the amended version of the Report of Committee 7. The reformers, harassed, as usual, by the itch to end the business, did not get all that they wished or might have sought in a more spacious opportunity. But my money is on version No. 2. What is more important, it was "welcomed" by Committee No. 7 and approved by the Preparatory Commission in Plenary Session, after immense labours by all.

Professor K. H. Bailey, of Australia, Chairman of the Drafting Committee, presenting the new version, said that "the aim of the Drafting Committee was to ensure that the form of presentation and the language used in the official documents of the United Nations should be simple and direct, and that formal traditional usages, which created a sense of artificiality and were confusing to the general public, should as far as possible be eliminated."

And this does not mean the general English-speaking public only. These documents begin in English, but travel the world in other tongues. What a compliment but what a responsibility! One most cheering feature of the affair is this—that the Chinese, French, Russian and Spanish delegates say that their labours will be lessened, their doubts diminished, and their own officials instructed and improved by such an exercise in simpler English. French "officialese," they tell me, is as bad as ours; and, for all I know, all the United Nations, to whom all these cosmic documents must go at last, may be as bad. What a fine thing that, from this poor bankrupt country this golden contribution to a Better World should go forth today! Finer still that the moving spirits in this battle for the English language should be—a Canadian and an Australian. . . .

28 December 1945.
To N. A. Robertson.
I had hoped before going away for a rest to write an introduc-

tion to the Report of the Canadian Delegation to the Preparatory Commission. This introduction would supplement the reports which have been prepared on each of the Committees. Since the Preparatory Commission closed I have not, however, had much energy, and so have been unable to prepare this. Before leaving for a week's rest tomorrow I have, however, dictated the attached memorandum which I will unfortunately not be able to see before this letter is sent off.

Comments on the work of the Preparatory Commission.[13]

Experience at the Preparatory Commission demonstrates that if Canada sends to a general international conference a competent and hard-working delegation, it becomes almost automatically one of the Big Five of the conference. French delegations at international conferences during 1945 have been tragically weak. The Scandinavian countries which used to play so large a role at Geneva are not yet able to send strong delegations, presumably because they need their best men at home for reconstruction. . . . The influence of the leading Powers at the Preparatory Commission was probably very much in this order:

> United Kingdom
> U.S.S.R.
> United States of America
> China
> Canada
> Netherlands
> Brazil
> Mexico
> Iran. . . .

The mixture of members of Parliament and of civil servants in the Canadian Delegation was a source of great strength. Members of Parliament who are good House of Commons men are able quickly to sense the feeling of an international meeting and to intervene at the right moment and in the right way. In the work of the Preparatory Commission their experience was of particular value in working out the Canadian revisions to the rules of procedure of the various organs. . . .

The results of the work of the Executive Committee and of the Preparatory Commission are definitely encouraging. Within six months of the signature of the Charter at San Francisco all 51 United Nations have ratified the Charter and have reached agreement on a bulky volume of recommendations, resolutions and reports. Unless some unforeseen event occurs the result will be that the various organs of the United Nations need spend only a day or so each rubber-stamping the recommendations of the Preparatory Commission. This means that in a day or so each organ will have adopted an agenda and provisional rules of procedure, and will have sent other parts of the Report to committees for further revision. The organs will thus be able to get down to their real business of dealing with questions of substance within a few days after they are set up. Had the Preparatory Commission not been held, or had it been, as was contemplated by most of the members of the Executive Committee, a formal conference to rubber-stamp the Executive Committee's Report, this happy event would not have been possible and the Assembly would have debated for at least four weeks on organizational questions.

The form which the Preparatory Commission took seems to have been the accidental result of the fact that one member of the Executive Committee (Mr. Reid) assumed that all the other members had the same idea of the Preparatory Commission as he had, namely that it would be a hard working conference which would be split up into sub-committees. Actually all the members seemed to have had the opposite idea, but when Mr. Reid incidentally mentioned his conception they rallied to it in the course of two weeks or so.

Much of the work which the Preparatory Commission did could have been done, and perhaps done better, by a small group of highly qualified officials got together by the Executive Secretary. This procedure would have been analogous to that followed by Sir Eric Drummond in the early days of the League. However, this procedure would not have had the same educational value which the Executive Committee and Preparatory Commission have had on those who participated in their work. The long arguments in the long committee sessions which went on for thirteen weeks in all were to a very great extent a discussion between the Soviet world and the Western world. If the Soviet Union had not been present, the Executive Committee and the Preparatory Commission could have done their work in about one-third of the time. But the long discussion has given the representatives of the

Western world a greater knowledge and understanding of the Soviet approach to international administration. Presumably it has
likewise given the Soviet representatives a greater understanding
of the way in which the minds of the representatives of the Western world work.

The Soviet who are always worried by the thought that they
do not possess persons who can compete on equal terms at international conferences with representatives of the Western world,
must feel as the result of the work of the last six months somewhat
more assured. Their delegations to the Executive Committee and
the Preparatory Commission were among the highest in the individual capacity of their delegates. Their international lawyers
topped all the other international lawyers present except Mr. Bailey of Australia. Moreover, their men have visibly grown in
ability—Mr. Gromyko and Mr. Roschin, for example, are now
much more able to hold their own in discussion without having
to fall back on the simple negative repeated monotonously for
three hours. . . .

One dominant theme in the first Assembly of the United Nations, as in all future Assemblies, will be the preservation of a
proper balance between the Assembly, the Security Council and
the Secretary-General. During the last six months it has become
clear that the powers of the Assembly are potentially larger than
was thought when the Charter was signed. Thus, though the
Charter explicitly gives the Assembly power only to establish regulations on the appointment of the staff of the Secretariat, the 51
United Nations have agreed to a report of the Preparatory Commission in which the General Assembly is requested to make recommendations concerning nearly every aspect of the work of the
Secretariat. This power flows from Article 10 of the Charter under
which the General Assembly may make recommendations on any
matter relating to the powers and functions of any of the organs of
the United Nations (subject to the one proviso contained in Article 12, which relates only to disputes and situations). Moreover
the Assembly derives a potentially enormous power because the
budget of the Organization must be approved by it, and in ap-
proving the budget it can settle for example the structure of the
Secretariat.

The interests of the Organization will be furthered by preserving intact all the implied as well as the explicit powers of the
Assembly, even though it may not be wise for the Assembly to

exercise all its powers immediately or in relation to certain matters. It is, therefore, suggested that Canadian Delegations to meetings of the organs of the United Nations should be instructed to resist an interpretation of the Charter which restricts the potential powers of the Assembly.

A decision will have to be made on how far the Canadian Delegation to the Assembly should go in pressing for the election of competent chairmen in the main committees. The Great Powers will prepare a slate of committee chairmen and expect it to go through automatically. This slate will probably contain a number of incompetents. Therefore it might perhaps be wise if Canada in consultation with a number of other responsible middle powers agreed in advance that there would be contested elections in all the main committees. . . .

The procedure to be followed in calling international conferences on trade and on health will occasion debate in the Assembly. A proposal was made late in the Preparatory Commission that instead of calling special ad hoc conferences on questions such as these an extraordinary session of the Assembly should be summoned to discuss each of the questions. This proposal was made too late to be examined thoroughly, but it would appear to offer obvious advantages. For one thing an extraordinary session of the Assembly called to draft an international trade convention would automatically have from its very first session an agreed set of rules of procedure. It would also have a staff experienced in handling an international conference. Moreover, the use of the Assembly for this purpose would increase the prestige of the Assembly, and would tend to develop its international legislative powers. There would also be less danger that an independent and unrelated agency would be established since the General Assembly, even though it might decide that a separate agency should be established for trade problems, would at the same time work out the agreement between that agency and the United Nations. . . .

Canada's chances of election to the Economic and Social Council are at the moment not good. We can scarcely hope for election unless we receive the support of most, if not all, of the Latin-American republics. These republics seem to be firmly convinced that a state which is a member of the Security Council ought not to be elected to the Economic and Social Council. They believe in the sharing of honours. In this attitude they appear to be supported by a considerable number of other delegations. It would seem that the best thing for us to do is to meet this argument head on in public in a speech in the General Assembly, and to support for membership in the Economic and Social Council states which have been elected to the Security Council.

At present we have a more than even chance of being elected to the Security Council, but it is possible that the theory of the distribution of honours may be applied even to our election to the Security Council on the ground that we are assured already of election to a very important body, the Atomic Energy Commission.

The chances of our being elected to these Councils will depend to a very marked degree on the calibre of the Canadian Delegation to the Assembly. Canada has been one of the Big Five of the Preparatory Commission. It is as much responsible as any other single nation for the contents of the Report of the Preparatory Commission, but unless Canada is represented by the strongest possible delegation in the Assembly, her past record may be a less important consideration than the theory of the distribution of honours. . . . Canada's chances of election will also of course be affected by the general position it takes in the Assembly in controversies between the Great Powers and the smaller powers. If Canada swings too much to the support of the Great Power positions it may lose more small power votes than it will gain from the votes of Great Power satellites. Dr. Victor Hoo of the Chinese Delegation was heard to remark sneeringly to some Latin-American Delegates after one of the debates on the site about "powers with a colonial mentality." When he saw a Canadian behind him he hastily explained that he was not referring to Canada, but his confusion was so evident that it is probable that he was. So far in the Executive Committee and the Preparatory Commission Canada has steered a middle course, and has been able on the merits of the questions which have come up to vote against the Great Powers about as frequently as it has voted with them. It is to be hoped that this happy situation will continue. [It didn't.]

31 December 1945. Monday.
4:15 p.m.
I decided that the best way to get a rest (especially since the Berkshire farm couldn't take me) was to go to a Canadian Army hospi-

tal. I got examined in London on Friday morning [28 December], got driven out Saturday morning and since then have been comfortably in bed in the officers' ward of No. 24 Canadian General Hospital at Horley in Surrey. . . . General Maurice Pope is next door. He got phlebitis but has been fixed up. I go in and chat with him from time to time.

The first thing they did when I got here was to X-ray my chest. I waited in the reception room for fifteen minutes for the report, feeling too tired to be worried. [My temperature was 102.4.] After fifteen minutes the major in charge came back shouting out so that all the room could hear—"You haven't got tuberculosis or cancer of the lungs." He then explained that if I'd had T.B. he would have had to send me to some other hospital.

A very nice doctor came in to see me in the afternoon. He asked a multitude of questions and tapped and probed me everywhere ending up with the statement that my own diagnosis was the correct one—that I was suffering from exhaustion—and what I needed was rest and extra food. When he was writing down my medical history he finished by asking me whether there was anything he hadn't covered. I said the only other thing was that every doctor told me that I was suffering from nervous tension. He said, "If you didn't have nervous tension you couldn't work so hard." Then when he took my blood pressure this morning he said, "I suppose you're always told that you have low blood pressure. That's one indication you'll probably live as long as your parents and grandparents. . . . "

The delegation to the Assembly is not as good as we'd hoped for. We'd hoped for the P.M., St. Laurent and [Brooke] Claxton. We got St. Laurent, [J. G.] Gardiner, and Paul Martin. However, we keep Graydon and Knowles who are both tops. [Stanley Knowles, C.C.F. M.P.]

This is the first New Year we have been separated for fifteen years. I hope it is the last. Last year was the pleasant evening [in Washington] with the Raushenbushes [Steve and Joan].

3 January 1946.
1:00.
To daughter Morna.
This living in a hospital is a funny life. . . . It's like sleeping on a conveyor belt where every few hours somebody has to adjust a

bolt or put some oil in you or dust you or something. Something's happening all the time. There's no rest for the patients. At seven the orderly comes in and wakes me. I open one eye, drink a glass of water and go to sleep. At 7:15 another orderly wakes me with my breakfast. This is more serious so I wake up enough to eat it. Then I try to go to sleep again but the nursing sisters (who are lieutenants) come in to make my bed and take my temperature. After they go I settle down again but the doctor, a nice major, comes in and asks me how I am. At 8:30 the orderly comes in with a cup of coffee; at 10:15 the nurse comes in with an egg-nog; by then I give up trying to go to sleep and decide to get up and have a bath and shave. Lunch comes at 11:30; tea at 2:00; they'll try to make me eat an egg-nog at 3:00 but I hide it and drink it after dinner which is about 4:30. Coffee and buttered toast and honey (lots of it) come at 8:30. Sleeping pills at 10:30 and I now find I can get a glass of milk then. So you see I am kept busy getting a rest.

6
The General Assembly
10 JANUARY–14 FEBRUARY 1946

In the first elections to the Security Council and the Economic and Social Council at the General Assembly in London in January 1946, the members of the U.N. paid more attention to equitable geographical distribution than to the ability of countries to contribute to the work of the councils. So far as the Security Council was concerned this was a clear breach of the provisions of Article 23 of the Charter which stipulated that the General Assembly, in electing the six nonpermanent members of the Security Council should give greater weight "to the contribution of members of the United Nations to the maintenance of international peace and security and to the other purposes of the Organization" than to "equitable geographical distribution." The other disturbing aspect of the voting was that the Latin-American and Arab members of the councils were selected by the caucuses of the Latin-American and Arab countries.

In September 1946, a month before the General Assembly was to resume its session in New York, the Canadian embassy in Washington transmitted to the State Department a memorandum I had written on elections to the councils. It set forth the Canadian opposition to "four undesirable conventions."

(1) The convention that the Assembly can properly disregard in elections to the Security Council the principle of functionalism set forth in Article 23 of the Charter;
(2) The convention that a state is ineligible for election to the Security Council if it is already a member of the Economic and Social Council;
(3) The convention that a number of regions of the world have a right to be represented on the Council by a state designated by them no matter what the qualifications of that state may be;

(4) The convention that only one member of the British Commonwealth, apart from the United Kingdom, should sit on the Security Council.[1]

What I feared would happen by the operation of these conventions did happen. Thus in 1956 the Latin-American members of the Security Council were Cuba and Peru. These were certainly not the Latin-American countries most able to contribute to the work of the Council. The Council was, of course, further weakened by the absence of China, since it could scarcely be argued that the representative appointed by the government in Taiwan represented China. This meant that the only representative in 1956 of the whole of Asia outside the Soviet Union was Iran. And this was the year of two simultaneous grave international crises, one precipitated by the British and French invasion of the Suez and the other by the Soviet suppression of the Hungarian Revolution.

In the elections to the Security Council in London in January 1946 Canada and Australia were both candidates. In the first ballot five countries received the required two-thirds majority: Brazil, Egypt, Mexico, Netherlands, and Poland. Canada was the sixth leading candidate but it secured only 33 votes, one less than a two-thirds majority. It lost because one of its supporters, Nicaragua, spoiled its ballot by signing it. The second ballot was confined to the two leading candidates which had failed of election on the first ballot, Canada and Australia. In this ballot, Australia secured 27 votes and Canada 23. In the next ballot the vote was 28 for Australia and 23 for Canada. Canada then retired from the contest.

The Canadian defeat came as a shock to the Canadian government. It had assumed that Canada would be elected, particularly since it and Brazil were the only countries supported by all five permanent members of the Security Council.[2] What Ottawa failed to recognize was the special place which H. V. Evatt, the foreign minister of Australia, had won at San Francisco for himself and his country among many of the smaller countries, especially the Latin-American, by his attacks on the great powers. Most Canadian politicians and officials at the San Francisco Conference had considered that these attacks were irresponsible. Irresponsible they may have been but they were popular. In December 1945 Eduardo Zuleta of Colombia, the president of the

Preparatory Commission, told Adlai Stevenson that there was support among all the Latin-American delegations for Evatt as president of the first session of the General Assembly. Zuleta, Stevenson reported, "talked at length about Evatt as a leader of smaller countries at San Francisco and the profound impression he had made upon all the Latin-American countries in this sense. For the same reason he said he thought Evatt would have a great deal of support among the smaller European countries."[3]

Paul Hasluck states in his memoirs that in the lobbying which he did in London in January 1946 to get Australia elected to the Security Council,

> perhaps the strongest point in favour of Australia was the expectation that she would be independent and not in the shadow of any one of the great powers. The reputation made at San Francisco by Evatt as the champion of the small powers still carried some weight. . . . We believed we had support from most Latin-American states, and from the Middle East, Iran, Turkey and Greece and possibly from Yugoslavia and Belgium.[4]

My feeling at the time was that if Canada had shown more independence of the great powers in the Preparatory Commission and the first session of the General Assembly it would have been elected to the Security Council. But in the Preparatory Commission we were forbidden by Ottawa to lead a campaign for detailed provisional rules of procedure for the Security Council which would have endeared us to most of the middle and smaller countries, and in the General Assembly we were so careful not to offend the great powers that I believe we alienated some of the middle and smaller countries. In my report to Ottawa on 28 December 1945 I had warned that this might happen.

7 January 1946. Monday.
4:00 p.m.
To Mother.
The devotees of Russia are, I am afraid, in for more disillusionment in the next five years or so than the devotees of any other major cult.

13 January 1946. Sunday.
9:45 p.m.
While I haven't had much to do since getting back to work I have
been feeling tired. I am gradually, however, getting back my
energy. I think also I am suffering from the release of tension now
that Hume Wrong has arrived and my responsibilities are slight.
It's also partly exasperation since Hume is pretty impermeable to
advice and lets advice flow over him at delegation meetings or sets
his jaw firm in private. We crossed swords in private several times
last week but lunched and dined amicably together today. Until
we were defeated in [the elections for] the Security Council Hume
poured cold water on all my proposals for our doing anything on
the ground they might cost us votes. Now we have lost with the
policy of caution, no one can prove we might not have won with a
policy of courage. I wanted us to meet the great powers head on by
opposing their very bad nominations for chairmen of committees,
to meet the Russians head on by fighting their efforts to get
around the rules for secret ballot on elections, and to vote for the
best possible candidates for the Economic and Social Council, regardless of the big power slates. I lost on all three and we maintained a dignified silence. . . .

15 January 1946.
Extracts from notes for speech by L. S. St. Laurent, chairman of
the Canadian delegation, in the opening debate in the General
Assembly.
        . . . The United Nations can realize its potentialities for
good only if its members refrain from exercising, save in the most
exceptional circumstances, their legal rights under the Charter to
veto, to withdraw from the Organization, and to plead domestic
jurisdiction. It is particularly important that the five permanent
members do not exercise, save in the most exceptional circumstances, their peculiar rights under the Charter. . . .
        If the United Nations is to grow in wisdom and strength it
must not be confined within the straightjacket of a rigid constitution. Its constitution—the Charter—must be capable of growth
and of adaptation to changing conditions without the necessity of
formal constitutional amendment, but by the development of custom and precedent. This means that the Charter must be
construed liberally and not restrictively. It also means that the

process of securing constitutional amendment—when amendments are needed—should not be too difficult.

The argument against rigidity in a document such as the Charter of the United Nations is particularly strong. No Charter drawn up in 1945 can be complete or final. The states and peoples of the world are, in setting up the United Nations, experimenting in many new fields of international cooperation. They are only at the beginning of their common experiment and they are experimenting and for some years will be continuing to experiment under peculiar conditions that are neither war nor peace. Not only will the Organization during its first few years exist in the twilight dawn between war and peace but its constitution was drawn up while the United Nations were still at war all over the world, while some governments were still in exile and others had only recently returned to their homelands, when millions of men were absent from their homes, and while hundreds of millions of men, women and children were tired in mind, body and spirit by the long years of war. The Charter was also drawn up before atomic bombs were dropped on Japan.

16 January 1946. Wednesday.
9:45 p.m.
The day before yesterday at a Dominions Office cocktail party I met again Sir Arthur Street, the second-in-command of the U.K. delegation at Chicago. [The international civil aviation conference held in Chicago in 1944.] He greeted me like a long-lost brother and said: "You and I are the only people who knew what was happening at Chicago."

18 January 1946. Friday.
10:20 p.m.
My mind is beginning to clear. It is still cotton wool but not quite as sodden a mass as it was before. By the time the Assembly is over it may be back half way to normal. Today I had Scotty Reston to lunch at the Travellers Club. I think he got a whole article out of me. It may perhaps appear in Sunday's *New York Times*. It is on the light which the Executive Committee and the Preparatory Commission threw on the nature of the schism between the Western world and the Soviet world. You might ask someone in the Department to look it up for you and to try to keep a copy for me. I

like Scotty very much and he seems to be fond of me. . . . I'm not really doing much worth while here. I think I'll make an agreement with Norman [Robertson] not to cover the same conferences as Hume [Wrong]. He makes a deliberate point of neither asking nor taking my advice. I give it anyway at delegation meetings— especially when he's not there when I usually win my case. My only exhausting job is the daily press conferences. They are becoming more and more popular. I like them when I have no cabinet ministers with me but not so much when I do. I try to interpret to the newspapermen what's happening and so far have not misled them though sometimes the news is pretty thin.

Hume is somewhat of a disappointment to me. He seems incapable of working as the organizer of a team. I know his worry was lest we should do anything to spoil our chances of election to the two Councils. I sympathize with his worries but he made no effort to share responsibility or to seek the advice of Dana or myself who ought to have some appreciation of the problem. Looking back on it I think we were right and he was wrong and moreover our suggestions would have been in the interests of the U.N. if carried out. I wanted us to give a speech in the Assembly attacking head-on the whole unhealthy tendency to distribute seats on the Councils and committee chairmanships on the basis of sharing honours and also attacking the great-power slates. I wanted us to vote for Iran for the Security Council even though it had no chance of election and I persuaded the delegation to support this position. Hume disregarded the decision and advised St. Laurent to vote for Egypt. If we had drummed up support for Iran we would have lost no votes since the Arab bloc voted against us anyway and we might have gained some votes. I wanted us to vote for Brazil and Mexico for the Economic and Social Council even though they had agreed with the other Latin republics that they were not candidates, because they ought to be members. We could have kept quiet, if necessary, so as not to offend the Latins. . . .

Hume asked Ritchie to do St. Laurent's speech [to the Assembly]. [I was disappointed because there was no trace in St. Laurent's speech of the notes for the speech which I had given Ritchie.]

20 January 1946. Sunday.
7:20 p.m.
We spend two hours this evening (8 to 10) doing a two-minute

movie [of a fake delegation meeting]. I am annoyed since it means I cannot go to a dinner Ken Bailey is giving for the Preparatory Commission's drafting committee and he says that without me the dinner will be Hamlet without the ghost.

In order to keep the record straight you can add to my grievances in the last letter that I urged that Canada and Australia should agree before the run-off vote was announced that the low man should withdraw; that when this was not done I urged we withdraw before a second vote. Our gesture would certainly have been the more effective the earlier it had come.

20 January 1946. Sunday.
To younger son, Timothy.
After lunch today we [an English cousin and I] went for a walk in Hyde Park. It has been very cold here for two days and the little lake in the Park which is called the Serpentine (why I don't know) had frozen over. The Serpentine is full of swans and geese so that some of the ice had been broken so that they could swim. When we got to the Serpentine I saw two big birds walking across the ice from the other side. They walked very clumsily like fat, waddling sailors on snow shoes. When they got closer we could see that they were swans. Swans are graceful when they are in the water but when they are out they are more awkward than almost any other form of animal life I have ever seen.

They very slowly and cautiously walked across until they were within a few yards of the open water. Then the older one slipped and couldn't get up again. He lay there with his feet stretched out just like a man on snow shoes who has fallen down and can't get up. His wife walked on a few more paces. Then she slipped and fell down. She was more agile than he so she managed to push herself along the ice on her belly till she reached the water and slipped in. She was so exhausted and thirsty that she put her long neck all into the water and took a great drink.

Mr. Swan by this time must have felt deserted by everyone and try as hard as he could he was only able to move about an inch a minute. However he finally got to the water—much to the relief of a couple of hundred people who were watching him.

28 January 1946. Monday.
9:30 p.m.
The Security Council is now taking all the limelight. So far I have

been able to get to all their meetings—today, disguised as a news-paperman. The issues are explosive—particularly now that the Iranian question is termed a dispute and the Soviet Union is deprived of a vote—but on the whole I think it is better this way than if the Security Council had had nothing important to do for the first months of its establishment. Bevin at Friday's meeting was belligerently tough. He had the burnt out stub of a cigarette (about ½ inch long) drooping from his mouth when he said—"I am so tired of charges made in private by the Soviet Government that no one will be happier than I shall be to see them brought out into the open." He didn't say anything today and I hope that when he speaks on Wednesday he will give a calm, judicial statement. Scotty Reston thinks the explosion on Friday was good but that Bevin should be cautious next time. The Security Council is playing with dynamite—Russia being put in the defendant's box at the first meeting—but it was unavoidable.

The Committee work is dull. For the most part the Committees are merely rubber-stamping the Preparatory Commission's report. I did more in a week in the Executive Committee to influence the future of the United Nations than the whole Canadian delegation will do in the four weeks of the Assembly. . . . 11:30 p.m. Just had a long talk with Hume on recent developments. Scotty Reston tells us that Mike's chances for the secretary-generalship are getting dim and that [Trygve] Lie of Norway will probably get the job. Scotty is depressed.

30 January 1946. Wednesday.
11:00 p.m.
I'm not doing much work. Attending a lot of committees as adviser or observer but that's about all. The Security Council meeting today was dramatic because no one knew what was going to happen. The resolution they passed on Iran was in the worst League jargon and tradition but Bevin's speech was magnificent. Nobody is very happy about the choice of Lie as Secretary-General. He seems to be no better than second-rate. He may not have enough courage or independence or integrity and he may also be subject to Soviet pressures exerted against Norway which is in a vulnerable position. Scotty Reston tells me that his qualifications were never discussed by the Security Council. The whole discussion was on equitable distribution of honours between North America and Europe and so on.

The only thing that amuses me now is the fight I am waging against Uno as the name of the United Nations. I show newspapermen a list of how other things would sound if that odious practice were followed—

Usa	(United States)
Uk	(United Kingdom)
Lon	(League of Nations)
Ilo	(Int. Labour Office)
Bit	(Bureau Int. du Travail)
Ussr	(USSR)
Ukssr	(Ukrainian S.S.R.)
Bssr	(Byelorussian S.S.R.)
Es	(El Salvador)
Nez	(New Zealand)
Phic	(Philippine Commonwealth)
Sa	(Saudi Arabia)

1 February 1946. Friday.
10:00 p.m.
I am so happy and excited by the thought that I'll be home with you in about ten days. Life is a little hectic sorting papers and getting ready for packing but I'm walking on air. It happened suddenly yesterday. Hume said he wanted to talk to me about going home. I said I had already jotted down the same thing to talk to him about, thinking that it was about time I got his permission to leave on the 14th. When we got to the office there was a wire from Norman [Robertson] suggesting I come home. Immediately we got Leo Malania busy on reservations. At first it looked hopeless since the sailing for the 7th was cancelled and the boats for the 3rd and 4th were full. Then Jimmy Gardiner cancelled his sailing on the 5th and I took it over. [James G. Gardiner, minister of agriculture.] I leave here 10:00 on Monday morning and we sail from Liverpool that night. . . . This will be my last letter to you for, I hope, a very long time. Seven months' absence is so unendurably long that I think I deserve a continuous seven months with you. Joseph's seven lean kine and seven fat kine.

7

Assessments

Rules of Procedure

At San Francisco, in London, and throughout the early years of the U.N., discussion of important questions of substance in the various organs of the U.N. was often frustrated by prolonged, confused, and acrimonious debates on questions of procedure. This was not surprising since the representatives of the various nations were accustomed to very different rules and conventions on procedure and each representative was convinced that the rules and conventions he was accustomed to were obviously sensible and had universal validity. Thus some representatives argued that before amendments to a resolution should be voted on, the resolution itself should be put to the vote. What was the sense, they would ask, of amending a resolution which was going to be defeated? Some argued that when several amendments were moved to a resolution, they should be put to the vote in the order in which they had been submitted. Others contended that the amendment farthest removed from the sense of the resolution should first be put to the vote and the others in order of their distance from the main resolution. If a resolution required a two-thirds majority, did an amendment to the resolution likewise require a two-thirds majority? What criteria should a chairman apply in deciding whether a resolution was procedural and thus requiring only a simple majority of the votes cast or substantive and requiring a two-thirds vote? Did one look only at the form of a resolution purporting to be procedural, or should one judge the resolution by what its effect would be if adopted? What was the procedure for suspending or amending a rule of procedure? Could this be accomplished by a resolution moved without notice and passed by a simple majority of the votes cast? When was it proper for a chairman to accede to a request by a delegate to reconsider a decision that had already been taken? After a vote had been taken could a delegate give a speech explaining his vote? Was a resolution to adjourn a debate or to close a debate or to question a chairman's ruling debatable? When were points of order in order? Could a chairman put a time limit on speeches after a debate had gone on for a long time?

One could go on and on listing the questions of procedure which led to prolonged wranglings in the U.N. in its early years. Sometimes in those early years I had the feeling that many delegates welcomed debates on procedure since these debates gave them opportunities to display their debating talents on issues on which they considered themselves to be expert. It was for them a relief from questions of substance on which they might feel inhibited from eloquence by lack of knowledge or by fear of offending a great power. Moreover, procedural points were often raised, especially by Soviet delegations or delegations controlled by them, to delay decisions in the hope—reasonable at times—that a decision delayed might be a decision averted.

Those of us on the Executive Committee who had been at the San Francisco Conference knew from bitter experience that if the General Assembly and the U.N. councils did not, at the very beginning of their existence, adopt precise and detailed provisional rules of procedure they would wallow in lengthy and exasperating debates on procedure. These debates would interfere with the speedy and effective discharge of their duties and would lower the prestige of the United Nations. The procedural debates in San Francisco had been held in private. The meetings of U.N. bodies would, with rare exceptions, be held in public. If the U.N. in public spent as much time in procedural debates as the San Francisco Conference had in private, the U.N. would be brought into contempt.

Much of our time in the committees of the Executive Committee and of the Preparatory Commission was therefore devoted to drawing up provisional rules of procedure for the General Assembly and the councils. The Secretariat of the Executive Committee (probably Andrew Cordier) produced a first draft of the rules for the Assembly and the Security Council based on the rules of the League of Nations. This was not admitted since it was feared with good reason that this would provoke the Soviet Union, which was determined to pretend that "there should be no implication that the United Nations organization is 'succeeding' to the League of Nations."[1] I circulated a revision of the Secretariat's drafts. After much debate we produced reasonably satisfactory provisional rules of procedure for the General Assembly, the Economic and Social Council, and the Trusteeship Council. Because of obstruction by the Soviet Union and the United States, supported fitfully by the other permanent members of the Security Council—Britain, France, and China—we were able to produce only curtailed and unsatisfactory provisional rules of procedure for the Security Council.

The opposition of the United States was caused in part by an unresolved conflict in Washington between the State Department and the Chiefs of Staff over the division of responsibility for American policy in the Security Council. Thus, at the beginning of the Preparatory Commission, the United States, as well as the United Kingdom members of the Preparatory Commission's committee on the Security Council, approved informally, in their personal capacities, the explanatory notes on the Council's rules of procedure which Canada had submitted; they also approved two amendments to the rules which had been recommended by the Executive Committee, one on secret balloting on the appointment of the secretary-general and the other on the suspension and amendment of the rules of procedure. Shortly afterwards the United States delegation received instructions from the Chiefs of Staff in Washington to resist any change in the rules recommended by the Executive Committee. The United States representative on the committee on the Security Council interpreted this instruction so literally that at one time he said in private to me that he could not accept the deletion of two whereases from the draft directive from the Security Council to the military staff committee.

The failure of the Preparatory Commission to recommend clear and precise draft rules of procedure for the Security Council was unfortunate, since the Security Council stood in greater need of such rules than the other organs of the U.N. The reason for this was that the chapter in the U.N. Charter on its central task of trying to promote the pacific settlement of disputes was badly drafted, and the provisions in the Charter on voting in the Security Council were obscure.

The chapter on peaceful settlement was indeed the most

badly drafted chapter in the Charter. The principal draftsman of this chapter (as indeed of much of the Charter) was Leo Pasvolsky of the State Department. Pasvolsky had a brilliant mind but he could not express himself clearly in writing, though he could in conversation. It was only when, as chairman of the Coordination Committee at San Francisco, he was repeatedly pressed by the members of the Committee to elucidate the obscurities in the chapter that the intent of the chapter (or at least his intent) became clear. The Coordination Committee agreed with his intent and tried to amend the chapter in order that it might express his intent clearly. Because of lack of time the Committee's desires were thwarted.

What the chapter did not make clear was that, with one exception, the only disputes or situations which the Security Council is authorized by the Charter to deal with are those it is obliged to deal with, namely those which are likely to endanger international peace and security. (The exception is when all the parties to a dispute request the Council to deal with it.) It follows from this that the first step the Council should take, once it decides to consider a dispute or situation, is to determine whether it is likely to endanger international peace and security. This may require an investigation by the Council. If the Council decides that the dispute or situation may endanger international peace and security it is under an obligation to take one or more of the following steps in any order it sees fit. It may remind the states concerned of their undertaking to settle their disputes by peaceful means. It may recommend to the states concerned that they adopt those particular peaceful means which the Council considers are most likely to be helpful. It may recommend terms of settlement. (I set forth this gloss on the Charter in the Canadian report on the San Francisco Conference.[2]) Precise rules of procedure for the Security Council could have clarified the meaning of the chapter on peaceful settlement.

Paul Hasluck, the Australian representative on the Executive Committee, has written about the struggle which he and I led in the Executive Committee for sensible provisional rules of procedure for the Security Council. He speaks of "the stubborn and fruitless hours" which we spent in argument.

The representatives of the smaller nations, and notably Mr. Escott Reid of Canada, produced argument after argument and made suggestion after suggestion, in an attempt to persuade the Committee that the development of practices and procedures [for the Security Council] was essential for the satisfactory working of the system of peaceful settlement and enforcement centred on the Security Council, and that the preparation of suggestions for the Council's future consideration would assist that end. . . . The records of the Executive Committee therefore contain quite a number of unregarded suggestions, including a comprehensive draft prepared by Mr. Reid, and the formal report of the Executive Committee contains in an appendix, as a sort of concession to the views of the smaller nations, a list of about fourteen subjects "which may ultimately have to be covered in the permanent rules of procedure of the Security Council." But all that the Preparatory Commission passed on to the Security Council was a very slim draft which contained rules of procedure on an inescapable minimum of subjects.[3]

At the very first meetings of the Canadian delegation to the Preparatory Commission held on 24, 25, and 26 November the question of the rules of procedure for the Security Council was discussed. Gordon Graydon, the leader of the Opposition in the House of Commons, believed that the delegation should press for detailed rules of procedure. He felt it would be unfair to leave the matter to the first eleven members of the Security Council since the rules of procedure would bind not only the first six nonpermanent members to be elected to the Council, but all the members of the U.N. which would sooner or later sit on the Council.[4] The delegation was, however, precluded from continuing the struggle for detailed rules of procedure for the Security Council which Canada had waged in the Executive Committee because it received a few days later an instruction from Ottawa that it was not to "press for the further elaboration of detailed rules of procedure . . . unless the permanent members of the Security Council themselves favour such a course." The telegram of instruction went on to say that "pressure for the elaboration of detailed rules of procedure . . . would be largely a waste of time as the Security Council is not likely in practice to allow itself to be bound by the recommendations of the Preparatory Commission."

The telegram was a toned down version of an informal note by Charles Ritchie of the Department of External Affairs, commenting on views I had expressed in a letter to Dana Wilgress, the Canadian ambassador in Moscow, on his appointment as head of the Canadian delegation to the Preparatory Commission.

> There is no use preparing elaborate documentation telling the permanent members [of the Security Council] how to behave like little gentlemen which they will toss out of the window when they meet. The agenda and procedure of the Security Council are political questions and cannot be considered as if they were rules for a girl's school. I hope Dana will not lend Escott support in making the Canadian delegation look silly by tilting at this windmill.[5]

When Ritchie contemptuously referred to rules for a girl's school he was probably influenced by the marginal comment which Hume Wrong had made on one of the rules which I had proposed to govern the conduct of members of the Council, "They can't be treated like school children."[6] They could, however, be treated like judges of the International Court of Justice and the language in my proposal to which Wrong took such violent exception was taken from the Statute of the International Court of Justice: "Members of the Court shall be bound, unless they are on leave or prevented from attending by illness or other serious reasons duly explained to the President, to hold themselves permanently at the disposal of the Court."

I found the argument in the telegram of instruction from Ottawa unconvincing at the time and I find it unconvincing today. A newly created organ of a newly created international institution cannot get down to business until it has adopted rules of procedure. If at its first meeting it is presented with a carefully considered set of provisional rules of procedure recommended to it by the member states of the institution of which it is an organ, it is highly unlikely that it will show contempt for those member states by tossing the set of provisional rules of procedure out of the window. Moreover it was not, as Ritchie seemed to suggest, the permanent members of the new organ who would make the decision. The decision of the Security Council would be made by all eleven members, and the decision, being procedural, would require an affirmative vote of any seven of them. The great power veto would not apply. There was therefore a reasonable chance—a chance in my opinion worth taking—that the Security Council would at its first meeting in January 1946 adopt provisionally the rules of procedure recommended to it by the Preparatory Commission even if they were detailed and even if some of the permanent members disliked some of them. The Security Council would presumably accompany this decision with a decision to set up a committee of experts to recommend to it as soon as possible a set of permanent rules of procedure.

Rules of procedure for the Security Council were, of course, as Ritchie wrote, political questions. But so were many of the other questions which the Executive Committee and the Preparatory Commission were dealing with. Nothing could be more political than the choice of a permanent headquarters for the U.N. The relations between the U.N. and the about-to-be dissolved League of Nations and the relations between the U.N. and the International Labour Organization were highly political questions. So was the organization of the U.N. Secretariat.

Ritchie may have been led into error by assuming, perhaps unconsciously, that the Preparatory Commission was the General Assembly in embryo and that it was improper for an embryonic General Assembly to recommend detailed rules of procedure to another principal organ of the U.N., the Security Council. But the Preparatory Commission was not the General Assembly in embryo. It was the heir of the San Francisco Conference. The San Francisco Conference was a constituent assembly of the U.N. Its task was to adopt a constitution for the U.N., called a charter. The Preparatory Commission was likewise a constituent assembly of the U.N. Its task was to supplement the constitution with draft constitutional statutes to be submitted to the organs of the U.N. once they were set up. One of those draft constitutional statutes should have been a set of precise and detailed provisional rules of procedure for the Security Council.

As soon as the Security Council started to meet it became clear that its effectiveness and its prestige were being diminished by its lack of detailed rules of procedure. Hasluck sat on the Council during the first four months or so of its operations. He wrote that up to May 1946

the Security Council has not succeeded in developing satisfactory practices and procedures and through the lack of them its work has often been impeded and confused. One of the most common complaints of the spectator at Council meetings is that, instead of talking about the substance of a case, the Council is always discussing procedural points. The complaint is well founded and most representatives on the Council would themselves confess to a sense of loathing and despair over the endless procedural wrangles that always seem to be getting in the way of their work. . . . [The Security Council] has not yet developed satisfactory techniques; it has not devised the methods of working that will give even a routine efficiency.[7]

I believe that if the government in Ottawa had given the Canadian delegation to the Preparatory Commission full backing in its efforts to provide detailed provisional rules of procedure for the Security Council, we might have succeeded. The Security Council would have started off as a more impressive and effective body. It might have continued as a more impressive and effective body. As the twig is bent so is the tree inclined.

Secretariat

Over Soviet opposition, the San Francisco Conference inserted provisions into the Charter which were not in the Dumbarton Oaks proposals and which set forth clearly the international character of members of the Secretariat. They were not to seek or receive instructions from any government. Governments of U.N. members were not to seek to influence them in the discharge of their responsibilities. The necessity of securing the highest standards of efficiency, competence, and integrity was to be the paramount consideration in the employment of the members of the Secretariat. It was only "due regard" which should be paid to the importance of recruiting staff on as wide a geographical basis as possible. In London the Soviet Union did its best, aided by some Latin-American states, to ensure that in the operation of the Secretariat the relative importance of these two criteria should be reversed: the paramount consideration should be equitable geographical distribution, and only due regard should be paid to efficiency, competence, and integrity. The Soviet Union also insisted that each member government have the right to veto the appointment of any of its nationals to the Secretariat. Indeed, what the Soviet Union obviously wanted was that all applications for employment or offers of employment in the Secretariat should be channelled through the foreign office of the potential member of the Secretariat. The Soviet Union also proposed in the Executive Committee that the Secretariat be divided into departments on organic rather than functional lines, so that the Security Council would have one department serving it, the Assembly, one department serving it, and so on. "Such a structure," I said at the time, in a report to Ottawa,

> would be inefficient since it would lead to unnecessary duplication of work in the political field; it would tend to divide the officials of the Secretariat between partisans of the Assembly and partisans of the Security Council; it would tend to diminish the role of the Assembly in the political and security field; it would tend to make the Security Council a thing apart from the rest of the Organization.

A compromise was arrived at. As a concession to the Soviet Union one department of the Secretariat was given the title "Security Council department." It was not, however, in fact a Security Council department since it served both the General Assembly and the Security Council on international political and security questions.

A good deal of what the Soviet Union and the other great powers failed to secure at San Francisco and in London they secured when the U.N. Secretariat was established in New York in the early months of 1946 by putting pressure on the first secretary-general, Trygve Lie, who was not strong enough to resist. Paul Hasluck, who represented Australia at the U.N. at that time, has written in his memoirs about this.

> The Secretary-General did not choose his assistant secretaries-general. The places were claimed by the powers. The five permanent members of the Security Council each had one and the others were given to one Latin-American, one Eastern European and one Western European. In my opinion three of the [eight] original appointments as assistant secretary-general were totally unsuitable, one was inadequate, two had modest but genuine qualifications and the assistant secretary-general for security affairs, though com-

petent, was first and foremost a nominee of the Soviet Union.[8]

The appointment of assistant secretaries-general who were totally unsuitable or inadequate, or who had only modest qualifications meant that it was difficult to get first-class men to serve under them. Difficult, but happily not impossible, for such men as Andrew Cordier, Ralph Bunche, and Brian Urquhart did agree to serve. But many of the original senior officers of the Secretariat had only mediocre abilities, and the blame for this must be shared between the governments which nominated inadequate assistant secretaries-general and Trygve Lie who accepted the nominations. The governments should have put forward no nominees or better nominees. Trygve Lie, even if he considered that he had to give in to the demands of governments to nominate assistant secretaries-general, should have made clear to them that, while he would hold open a post of assistant secretary-general for each great power and for each of the three groupings of powers (Latin-America, Eastern Europe, Western Europe), he would not fill that post until the government or governments concerned had made a first-class man available for it.

A first-class secretary-general such as Dag Hammarskjold would have done this. But Trygve Lie was not first-class. Immediately after his election, I wrote in a letter to my wife on 30 January 1946:

> Nobody is very happy about the choice of Lie as Secretary-General. He seems to be no better than second-rate. He may not have enough courage or independence or integrity and he may also be subject to Soviet pressure exerted against Norway which is in a vulnerable position.

The United States and British governments when they concurred in his appointment knew he was not first-class. Dean Acheson said before his appointment that he did not consider him a very impressive candidate.[9] Philip Noel-Baker was very much disturbed over the prospect of Lie being selected; in his opinion he was all right in Norway, where he was quite a good foreign minister, but he was not nearly quick enough or astute enough to tackle the work of secretary-general. Noel-Baker wanted Ernest Bevin to support a last-minute move to draft Eisenhower for a couple of years, with the hope that Pearson would succeed him.[10]

An Approach to Some of the Basic Problems of Foreign Policy,
9–11 February 1946

I had a very comfortable cabin on the ship on which I returned to Canada in February 1946, and I spent much of my time
there sorting out my ideas and putting them down on paper. The
result was the following memorandum. I gave this memorandum
to the four most influential officers of the Department of External
Affairs—Robertson, Wrong, Pearson, and Wilgress.

1. The basic problems of foreign policy which today confront any
state arise in the main out of two developments: the discovery of
the atomic bomb and of other methods of massive destruction,
and the schism between the Soviet world and the Western world.
2. "A weapon has been developed that is potentially destructive
beyond the wildest nightmares of the imagination; a weapon so
ideally suited to sudden unannounced attack that a country's major cities might be destroyed overnight by an ostensibly friendly
power." (Atomic Energy: a general account of the development of
methods of using atomic energy for military purposes under the
auspices of the United States Government, 1940–1945, Page 134.)
3. The schism between the Soviet world and the Western world
has its roots deep in the past: the schism between Orthodox Christendom and Catholic Christendom, the division of Europe between the Slav and the Western European, the difference between
a state which has expanded over a land mass and states which have
expanded overseas. The schism which was already great in 1914
has been widened by the revolution of 1917 which dispossessed a
westernized upper class and which resulted in the establishment
in Russia of a totalitarian, socialistic, nationalistic and expan-
sionist state which has successfully insulated its people from the
currents of thought and feeling in the Western world. Each of the
worlds is profoundly suspicious and fearful of the other.
4. The Soviet world is not a purely geographical unit. Within the
boundaries of the Western world are members of the Soviet
world—people, mainly communist, whose loyalty is not to a
Western nation state or to the Western world but to the Soviet
world.
5. The communists are not the only people who are *in* the Western world but not *of* it and who are in this sense members of the

proletariat of the Western world. The coloured and colonial peoples are also members of that proletariat as are others who feel, because of spiritual malaise or material misfortune, that they are not part of the community in which they live. There is thus a schism within the Western world and the Soviet world is trying to organize and command the schismatics.

6. The geographical boundary between the Soviet world and the Western world is unstable. This is largely due to the weakness of most of the states which border the Soviet world. These states are, for the most part, poverty stricken and badly and corruptly governed. China, India and the countries of the Middle East have, moreover, only recently been brought within the Western world and the process of westernization has affected only a small upper class. China's hold over its border territories of Manchuria, Sinkiang and Tibet is weak as is Iran's hold over its border territories. Moreover the social and economic advance of the Soviet border republics in the Far and Middle East and their relative cultural freedom is proving a magnet to the corresponding nationalities on the other side of the border, most of which have legitimate cause for discontent with their present lot.

7. The whole world has been weakened by two destructive bouts of war in thirty-one years. These wars have killed off many of the potential creative leaders in each community. Others who might have been creative leaders are tired in mind, body and spirit. Others are so baffled and bewildered by events that they are playing truants from the task of trying to find an adequate answer to the problems which confront us: they seek refuge from reality in pleasure or in the daily round, the common task, in cynicism or in philosophic detachment.

8. Others have weighed the problem of how in an atomic age to preserve peace between the Soviet world and the Western world and have concluded that the problem is insoluble. They can see no end except an atomic war.

9. The chances may be 100 to 1 or even 1000 to 1 that this atomic war is what we are headed for. The consequences of that war would, however, be so disastrous—whichever side won—that we must try our best to prevent the disaster even if our chances of success are only 1 in a 1000.

10. There would seem to be three possible approaches to a solution of the problem and these three approaches should be ex-

plored simultaneously. The first is to try to reach by peaceful means a less unstable geographical equilibrium between the Soviet world and the Western world. The second is to try to end the schisms within the Western world. The third is the longer, slower process of trying to end the schism between the Western world and the Soviet world.

11. These approaches are not sharply distinct from each other. Thus the more nearly the schisms within the Western world are ended the stronger will the Western world be and the less it will have to give way to the Soviet world before a fairly stable equilibrium is reached.

12. The securing of a less unstable geographical equilibrium between the two worlds means that we must resign ourselves to an extension of Soviet influence over border territories especially in the Middle East. We should, however, do our best to ensure that this extension is done at as little cost in human suffering and moral values as possible and that it is done as slowly as possible so that, while fighting a rearguard action, we can build up our defences behind us by strengthening the economies of the next line of border territories, by linking their economies with ours, by forcing reforms in corrupt and inefficient administrations in these territories and by meeting the grievances of their peoples against their own governments and those of the Western world.

13. The ending of the schisms within the Western world will be a long and slow process. To protect us while we are undertaking this task we should try to disillusion the Western proletariat about the good faith of the Soviet agents who are trying to capitalize on their discontents. One way of doing this is to demonstrate that local communist parties are agencies of a foreign power and instruments of the foreign policy of that power—a foreign policy which serves the interests of the governing class of the Soviet world not the interests of the proletariat of the Western world. Another way is to spread disillusionment about the Soviet world by encouraging the telling of the truth about present tendencies in the Soviet world towards class distinctions, class barriers, social inequality and the creation of hereditary classes.

14. These are however short-run expedients. An enduring solution can be found only if the states of the Western world pursue policies of high and stable levels of employment, reduce disparities in income, increase equality of opportunity, increase freedom

for colonial peoples, reduce and ultimately eliminate inequalities based on colour or race.

15. No simple prescription can be written out for ending the schism between the Western world and the Soviet world. If the two worlds live side by side in peace for many years they will, however, tend to become more and more similar. But we cannot be content to trust to this natural tendency alone. In the first place the problem of narrowing the schism is too urgent since as long as the schism is wide the danger of a devastating war is imminent. The natural tendency of the two worlds to become less unlike each other must therefore be speeded up. In the second place we must care and care deeply about the kind of common goal to which the two worlds will tend to move. If they should both absorb the worst from each other our last state would be worse than our first. Not only would most of the cultural, intellectual and spiritual fruits of six thousand years of civilization be lost but we should not even have attained peace, for should the nations of the Western world become totalitarian, parochial, nationalist, socialist and tribal worshipping they would become like the Soviet world but they would also be irreconcilable with each other and with the Soviet world since each state would refuse to recognize any higher object of worship than itself.

16. In order to end the schism in a way which will bring us peace and preserve the values of civilization we must first be clear about the nature of the schism. The schism is a moral schism which has to do with the relation of the individual man, woman and child to the community and the state. The essence of the Western Christian faith is that the individual is eternal and the state and the community are temporal. The individual is an end in himself. The state and the community are mere means by which the individual may be helped to attain the good life. Opposed to this faith is the totalitarian heresy that whatever serves the interests of the state or the community is right. (Salus populi suprema lex.) "The tribe is the tribesman's spiritual absolute and therefore the worship of the tribe is the highest form of religion that a human being can have." (Toynbee, A. J. "A Study of History". Vol. V, page 79.) The heresy remains a heresy whether the tribe numbers a few hundred people or embraces the whole population of the world.

17. In order that the schism may be ended without in the process destroying the values of civilization the Western world must con-

vert the Soviet world from its heresy. In order to prevent war we must launch a war for men's minds. We cannot win that war unless we are convinced of the truth of our gospel, unless we practise it, unless we preach it with fervour. In so far as we practise it we shall find ourselves adopting what is best in the tradition of the Soviet world—economic equality, economic democracy, cultural autonomy, the abolition of classes and the withering away of the police state. ["Creed" would have been a better word than "tradition."] The Western world will not only have put an end to its own internal schisms but will also have gone half way to meeting the Soviet world on common ground.

18. Three possible approaches to the solution of the problem of how to preserve peace in an atomic age between the Western world and the Soviet world have been outlined: to try to reach by peaceful means a less unstable geographical equilibrium between the two worlds; to try to end the schisms within the Western world; to try to end the schism between the two worlds. The United Nations is one of the instruments which can be used in pursuing these policies.

19. The Security Council and the General Assembly can be used (as the Council was in the Soviet-Iranian dispute in January 1946) to strengthen the bargaining position of a border state which is under pressure from the Soviet Union and thus slow down the rate of Soviet expansion. The Security Council and the General Assembly also provide forums in which the Western world can preach its own gospel and attack the heresies of the Soviet world. This propaganda may have some effect on the schismatics in the Western world. Its main value will, however, be that it will increase the faith of the Western world in itself.

20. In order to be successful the faith of the Western world must show itself in good works. In the Trusteeship Council the Western world must take the initiative away from the Soviet world and must press for a rapid realization of the ideal of independence for non-self-governing peoples. This policy is risky, but less risky than letting the Soviet Union get away with posing as the defender of colonial peoples and using anticolonialism as a wedge to divide the United States from Great Britain, the Netherlands and France.

21. The Economic and Social Council and the specialized agencies must be used to the limit by the Western world as instruments

for attaining as rapidly as possible high and stable levels of employment, rising standards of living, and greater economic equality within states and between states. Successful pursuit of these policies will narrow the schisms within the Western world by reducing the number of the discontented proletariat. Since the successful pursuit of these policies will depend in the main on increasing cooperation between the states of the Western world (and only to a very limited extent on cooperation with the Soviet world) the successful pursuit of the policies will tend to unite the states of the Western world and thus strengthen their hand in dealing with the Soviet world.

22. In the General Assembly and in the Economic and Social Council an immediate drive should be made to formulate a declaration of the rights and duties of states and a declaration of the rights of man. These two documents can become the creeds of the Western world—its articles of religion. If the campaign is handled well, if, for example, the drafts put forward as a basis of discussion are sensible, the Soviet world will be put on the defensive and will find it difficult to refuse to sign the declarations. Once they have signed we have a new weapon to use in our war for the minds of the citizens of the Soviet world.

23. The Secretariat of the United Nations should be consciously used as an instrument for sowing doubt in the minds of at least a few citizens of the Soviet world about the orthodoxies in which they have been brought up. The Soviet world should be given its fair share of appointments to the higher posts in the Secretariat. We should encourage the appointment of nationals of the Soviet world as probationers in the middle and lower ranks where they will be given in-service training. It would be most valuable, for example, if up to one-third of the lower ranks—stenographers, typists, accountants, elevator men, messengers, etc.—came from the Soviet world. The mere fact that these were ordinary people would mean that a little light about the West might percolate through to the ordinary people of the Soviet Union.

24. A further set of considerations should be taken into account in deciding how best to use the United Nations as an instrument of the foreign policies of the states of the Western world. The goal of the threefold approach to the present problems of foreign policy is, of course, peace. Constitutionally that goal means world government. The time it will take us to get world government will be

diminished if we consciously pursue within the United Nations policies likely to lead to world government. Therefore when there is a choice between alternative policies we should support that one which is the more likely to speed up the trend to world government.

25. It is, for example, desirable that the General Assembly should gradually become a true international legislature. This means that we want it to have as its major task the adoption of conventions for submission to member states for ratification. The Assembly and not *ad hoc* diplomatic conferences should pass this international legislation. Therefore, instead of holding *ad hoc* conferences on such matters as trade, health, etc., special sessions of the Assembly should be summoned to deal with these problems. Before being submitted to the Assembly the legislation will, of course, have to be drafted. The drafting of the legislation ought to be the job of the appropriate commission or committee of one of the three Councils or of a subsidiary organ set up by the Assembly. A commission, committee or subsidiary organ would be assisted by the Secretariat and would include in its membership, or consult with, the states principally concerned in the problem.

26. Similarly, it is desirable that the International Court should become a true judicial body. This means that the Court should have jurisdiction over all [legal] disputes between states, i.e., the optional clause should be obligatory.

27. The development of the world state means the drastic reduction and limitation of national armaments, and effective international inspection of national armaments. It means creating a cosmopolitan international police force, the abolition of the great power veto, the withdrawal of the reservation on domestic jurisdiction and the establishment of weighted voting in the Assembly. Developments which will lead in this direction should therefore be supported. [Under weighted voting, instead of each member state having one vote regardless of population, a member state would have a number of votes which reflected its ability to contribute to the maintenance of international peace and security, as well as to other purposes of the U.N.]

28. The policies of each of the states of the Western world in the United Nations should be consciously based on the paramount importance of using the United Nations to attain the objectives outlined above. Other considerations—national prestige, partic-

ular national advantage—are of minor importance, so minor as not to be worth paying attention to in any realistic pursuit of long-run national interests. Under any rational calculation of the odds the chances of preventing an atomic war are slight. Yet, unless that war is prevented, most of the things worth caring for will disappear. Therefore, the overriding consideration in determining every decision on foreign policy must be the prevention of that war. Wisdom alone will not prevent the war. Wisdom must be accompanied by courage and integrity.

Impressions of the First General Assembly

25 February 1946.
To Hume Wrong.
I would suggest a rewording of paragraphs 5 and 6 [of your draft memorandum][11] on impressions of the first General Assembly somewhat as follows:

> The Soviet delegations used the Security Council, the General Assembly and its committees as platforms from which to launch a propaganda campaign to demonstrate that they are the defenders throughout the world of the rights of labour, of colonial peoples and of small nations. They must have done this under instructions from the Soviet Government. They met with considerable success in their efforts and it can be assumed that they will continue these tactics at future meetings of the organs of the United Nations. They forced controversial issues such as the World Federation of Trade Unions and war criminals on the agenda of the General Assembly and made the most of other controversial issues which were already on the agenda or were put on the agenda by other countries. They might not have taken the initiative in raising controversial issues in the Security Council but when the Iranian dispute was raised they countered with the controversial issues of Greece and Indonesia and made the most of them as well as of the complaint of Syria and the Lebanon. . . . The Soviet delegations used the London sessions of the United Nations in much the same way as an opposition party uses the sessions of parliament in a democratic country. Their arguments were addressed not so much to the

delegates in front of them as to their constituents—the peoples of the world. The Soviet at Dumbarton Oaks and San Francisco tried to impose extreme limitations on the powers of the General Assembly to discuss important questions fearing that the General Assembly would be used against them. Soviet policy has been to keep important issues off the Security Council until the Big Three had come to agreement on them. Having lost their fights on these two points they have now with their usual realism decided to use the Assembly and the Security Council as instruments of their foreign policy and instead of remaining on the defensive and merely resisting attacks levelled at them they have gone over to the offensive. This came as a surprise to most delegations in London which had not expected the Soviet to fight in London the first round of the battle of the new psychological warfare. Clearly the states of the Western world will now have to meet these tactics by going over to the offensive themselves by using the organs of the United Nations as instruments of their foreign policy, particularly in the field of psychological warfare. On the whole this tendency will strengthen the United Nations in the long run since it will tend to make the organs of the United Nations into bodies similar in this respect to national legislatures. The difficulty, of course, from the point of view of Western powers is that as long as the borders of the Soviet Union remain closed to outside propaganda they find it almost impossible to get their propaganda, launched at meetings of the United Nations, across to the peoples of the Soviet states, but they can at least get their arguments across to the border states and to Soviet sympathizers in the Western world. . . .

I am doubtful about the concluding sentence of your memorandum, even though it states only that the question whether the establishment of the United Nations has in fact furthered the maintenance of international peace and security is an "open" one. Perhaps that is because I am an interested party having invested the better part of a year in the Organization. In order to say that the question is open you must be able to argue that the present situation would be no worse if the United Nations had not been established. Is it possible to maintain this? Presumably the "attitude towards each other of the great powers" would have been about the same if the United Nations had not existed. They would either have continued to meet at five or three-power meetings and quarrelled (with the quarrels getting out into the press) or they would not have met and would have quarrelled through diplomatic channels and by open Soviet abuse in their press and radio countered by public statements by the leaders of the Western powers. So far as I can judge the quarrels would have gone on anyway, and the existence of the United Nations has not made them worse. On the other hand the existence of the United Nations has already done some good and may do much more good in matters not directly related to their quarrels.

Standing Instructions to Canadian Delegations to Meetings of the U.N., 26 February 1946

It would be useful if agreement could be reached on comparatively brief standing instructions for Canadian delegations to meetings of the organs of the United Nations and of specialized agencies. This standing set of instructions would, of course, be revised from time to time in the light of experience. For the purposes of each meeting it would be supplemented by a special set of instructions for that meeting. One advantage of such a standing set of instructions is that it would set forth in as precise terms as possible the policy of the Canadian Government on those general issues which are likely to arise at most if not all meetings. Agreement on such a set of instructions would make it possible for the special instructions for a conference to be less detailed. This would give a delegation the necessary freedom of action to apply the general principles to the specific issues which arise, many of which cannot be foreseen in advance. The attached memorandum [below] is a tentative first draft of such a set of instructions. . . .

1. Disregard calculations of the possible immediate effect of pursuit of a given policy on the number of votes which Canada is likely to secure in elections and base policy on what seems to be in the best long-run interests of the United Nations and of Canada.

There are two arguments for this proposition. The first is that national prestige and immmediate national advantage are of little importance compared with the long-run interests of Canada in preventing another war; one of the instruments which can be used in preventing that war is the United Nations. The second is that in the long run Canada's chances of getting votes in the United Nations would be greater if, by its actions in the United Nations, Canada earns the reputation of pursuing an undeviating course in the United Nations in what it considers to be in the long-run interests of the Organization; Canada is in a weak position in bargains between blocs, its claim to election on the basis of equitable geographical distribution will usually be slight and its best chance of election will probably therefore be if it earns the respect of the members of the United Nations.

2. Emphasize the importance in the interests of the United Nations of adhering to the principle of functionalism in elections to the Councils and to similar bodies.

Unless the Councils and similar bodies include the states which have the greatest contribution to make to the solution of the problems with which they have to deal they will not be able to do the most effective work.

3. Oppose selection of members of the Councils and of similar bodies by regional groups.

In London in January 1946 Latin-American Republics chose the states from among them which should sit on the Security Council and on the Economic and Social Council and they also designated their representatives for the General Committee. The Arab states did much the same thing and both blocs were successful in having their candidates elected. If this practice is continued the Councils will not in fact be elected by the Assembly but the Assembly will merely ratify the decisions of regional groups. In the First Assembly this practice, along with devotion to the principle of the sharing of the honours, resulted in the two Latin-American Republics (Brazil and Mexico), which had most to contribute to the work of the Economic and Social Council, being left off that Council and the Arab bloc being represented on that Council by Lebanon. It is difficult for regional blocs to resist the pressure for rotation with the result that the Councils will become weaker and weaker bodies as time goes on. Moreover the use of the bloc system at elections results in a number of states being disbarred from membership in the Councils since they do not belong to any particular bloc.

4. Assist the more responsible Latin-American states, such as Brazil and Mexico, in fighting against a solid Latin-American bloc.

Brazil is seriously concerned about the dangers in the long run of the Latin-American Republics casting solid votes at international conferences. Since it considers itself a marginal great power it is also opposed to the principle of rotation among the Latin-American Republics. Close relations should therefore be established at a conference between the Canadian and Brazilian delegations so that Brazil may let us know when we can be of assistance to it in this matter.

5. Establish a close working relationship with the other middle powers: Brazil, Mexico, the Netherlands, Belgium, Czechoslovakia, Australia, India (and Poland if it secures reasonable freedom of action).

Experience has demonstrated that, in general, the interests of the middle powers coincide more with the general interest than do the interests of the small powers or of the great powers.

6. Press for the election of chairmen of the working committees and of sub-committees on the basis of their personal competence to conduct the meetings expeditiously and well.

Most of the constructive work at an international meeting is done in committees and sub-committees. They are the creative bodies on the success of which a conference depends. The chances of a committee doing constructive work increases in direct proportion to the competence of its chairman. Incompetent or unscrupulous chairmen will snarl the work of the committee and lower the prestige and effectiveness of the United Nations.

7. Insofar as slates for Councils, chairmanships, etc. are not in accord with the principles set forth above, they should be disregarded and the Canadian delegation should openly announce its opposition to them and, if necessary, put forward in public its alternative slate.

8. Fight against the settlement of issues of general interest behind the scenes by the Big Three or the Big Five.

The danger of such settlement behind the scenes is that the Big Three or the Big Five will support in full conference the policy demanded by the most obstinate of them; the result will be that discussion in full conference will be a sham since the members of the Big Three or Big Five who have been bludgeoned into supporting a policy of which they disapprove will be unable to discuss in full conference the real issues involved.

9. Defend the independence of the international Secretariat against improper pressure by individual member states and demand strict adherence to Article 100 of the Charter on the independence of the Secretariat and to Article 101(3) which makes the *"necessity* of securing the highest standards of efficiency, competence and integrity" a *"paramount* consideration" and makes equitable geographical distribution only an "important" consideration to which vague "due regard" should be paid.

10. Press for effective discussion at each September meeting of the General Assembly of the report by the Security Council on the measures which it has "decided upon or taken to maintain international peace and security."

It is in the interests of the Organization that the concurrent powers of the Assembly to deal with political and security questions should be maintained unimpaired and that the members of the Security Council in making their decisions should always be aware of the fact that they may have to defend their decisions before the General Assembly. Discussion in the Assembly of the work of the Security Council, in order to be effective, will have to be carried on by a small subcommittee of the Assembly's main committee on political and security questions. It may be found desirable to turn this small sub-committee into a subsidiary organ of the Assembly as the Netherlands has proposed.

11. Press for the formulation and adoption as soon as possible by the General Assembly of a declaration of the rights of man and a declaration of the rights and duties of states. If possible these declarations should be cast in a form in which it will be necessary for the member nations to bring them before their legislative bodies for ratification. They might even be in the form of amendments to the Charter.

The Soviet states have demonstrated that they intend to use the organs of the United Nations as instruments of Soviet propaganda in a war for men's minds. Already they have met with success in their efforts to pose as defenders of the rights of small nations and of coloured and colonial peoples. The

Soviet states will win the battle for men's minds if the Western world remains on the defensive. The Western world should, therefore, go over to the offensive and should attack the Soviet states at their weakest point—their refusal to concede to their citizens the ordinary freedoms of speech, of the press and of worship, and their inability to give their citizens freedom from want and from fear. The Soviet states are also on the defensive in that they in recent years have been more guilty of offences against the rights of other states than have the states of the Western world. They are in a particularly embarrassing position so far as a declaration of the rights and duties of states are concerned since such a declaration could be based almost in its entirety on proposals made to the League of Nations by Soviet representatives.

12. Press for consideration by the General Assembly of the "principles governing disarmament and the regulation of armaments" and for the making of recommendations on the implementation of these principles.

At the moment it seems that the Soviet states are less willing to disarm than are the states of the Western world and that they would be less willing to submit to effective international inspection and regulation of their armaments. On the other hand, in the inter-war period they pressed more vigorously than any other states for the limitation of armaments. Consequently they would be put on the defensive if the Western world were to press now for disarmament and the effective regulation of armaments. Discussion at the General Assembly of this question will, in order to be effective, have to be carried on by a small sub-committee of the main committee on political and security questions. It may be found desirable to make this small sub-committee into a subsidiary organ of the General Assembly so that it will remain in existence between sessions of the Assembly.

13. Press for the encouragement by the General Assembly of "the progressive development of international law and its codification."

This too will tend to put the Soviet states on the defensive. The Assembly should probably set up a subsidiary organ for the purpose of encouraging the progressive development and codification of international law.

14. Encourage the development of the General Assembly into an

international legislative body. This means that, save in exceptional circumstances, general multilateral conventions should in future be adopted by the Assembly rather than by *ad hoc* international conferences. It also means that the main job of each Assembly should be the passage of these conventions and that the main job of the Economic and Social Council should be the drafting of international legislation for submission to the Assembly.

15. Encourage discussion in the General Assembly of the desirability in the near future of introducing weighted voting in order to make it a more democratic and effective body.

16. Support a restrictive interpretation of the veto rights of the Great Powers.

17. Support a restrictive interpretation of the reservation of domestic jurisdiction.

18. Support an extensive interpretation of the powers of the General Assembly under Article 10 of the Charter which gives it an unrestricted grant of power to make recommendations to the members of the United Nations and to the Security Council on any question or matter (other than a dispute or situation which is being dealt with by the Security Council) which is within the scope of the Charter or which relates to the powers and functions of the Security Council, the Secretariat, the Court or any other organ of the United Nations.

19. Support an extensive interpretation of the rights and duties of the Secretary-General under Article 99 of the Charter to "bring to the attention of the Security Council any matter which, in his opinion, may threaten the maintenance of international peace and security."

The restrictive interpretation of this Article, which has been that favoured by the Soviet states, is that this merely gives the Secretary-General a reserve power in emergency to put a question on the agenda of the Security Council. The extensive interpretation is that the Secretary-General may bring a matter to the attention of the Security Council by, if necessary, intervening in the discussion by the Security Council.

20. Support an extensive interpretation of the rights and duties granted to the various organs of the United Nations under the Charter and maintain that where a right or duty is granted explicitly or implicitly to the Organization and is not assigned to any specific organ it has been granted to the General Assembly.

21. Support an extensive interpretation of Chapter XI of the Charter which is the declaration regarding non-self-governing territories.

Up to the meeting of the General Assembly in January 1946 the colonial powers, including the United Kingdom, tended to take the line that this Chapter was no more than a unilateral declaration by each colonial power; that it therefore gave rise to no international obligation and did not give the Organization the right to enquire into whether the colonial powers were, in fact, living up to their declaration. The extensive interpretation is that this declaration, being embodied in the Charter, gives rise to a treaty obligation and that the Organization, therefore, has the right to enquire into the question whether the colonial powers are living up to their pledges and that the Assembly may make recommendations to the colonial powers on how they may more speedily give effect to their pledges. This extensive interpretation is supported by the United States and the Soviet states and, unless the colonial powers are to be put on the defensive by the Soviet states, it would be wise for them to support an extensive interpretation from which the respectable colonial powers, such as the United Kingdom, have nothing to fear.

22. Resist efforts to limit the power of the General Assembly to control the Secretariat.

Because of their own constitutional tradition based on the theory that legislative and executive powers should be divided, some of the United States representatives, especially those from the Bureau of the Budget, tend to take the line that the Secretary-General should be left free from what they call interference by the General Assembly. They argue that Article 101 (1) of the Charter gives the Assembly merely the power to establish regulations under which the Secretary-General appoints the staff and does not give the Assembly power to make recommendations on the structure of the Secretariat and on its internal regulation. Constitutionally this argument is bad since it disregards the content of Article 10 of the Charter and also the Assembly's power to control the Secretariat through its control of the budget. The argument of substance against the United States position is that a Secretary-General, who is left free of direction by the General Assembly, will not, in fact, be a free agent but will be subjected to pressure by the Big Powers and especially by the Soviet Union. The General Assembly can protect the Secretary-General against such pressure by establishing extensive rules and regulations on the Secretariat and by making recommendations to the Secretary-General on the Secretariat.

23. Remain in the forefront of the struggle to develop the most satisfactory possible rules of procedure for the various organs. These rules should be kept under continuous review in order that they may be perfected and that they may, as far as possible, be identical and in simple language. The General Assembly should, if necessary, assert its right to make recommendations to the Security Council on the revision of the Security Council's rules of procedure.

The better the rules of procedure of the various organs are the more effective the work of the organs will be and the less the danger that their prestige will be lowered by disputes and delays over procedural matters. The more nearly identical the rules of procedure of the various organs are the easier it will be for delegates to participate effectively in discussions since they will not have to learn a new set of rules of procedure for each organ. For this reason it is also desirable that the rules of procedure of the specialized agencies, particularly those rules dealing with the conduct of business, should be, as far as possible, identical with the rules of procedure of the organs of the United Nations.

24. Remain in the forefront of the struggle to simplify the form and language of reports, recommendations, resolutions, conventions and other documents.

The use of old fashioned form and language for United Nations documents erects an unnecessary barrier between the United Nations and the ordinary citizen. It makes the documents less forceful and less readable. It also makes it easier for organs to pass resolutions with little or no content in them.

Sources and List
of Works Cited

My letters to my wife from April 1945 to February 1946 constitute the principal source of this book. These letters will eventually be deposited with other papers of mine in the Public Archives of Canada. I have supplemented these letters with papers in folders 7 and 8 of my "External Affairs Papers" in the Public Archives and with papers in the files of the Department of External Affairs of Canada which are now in the Public Archives. The files of the Department of External Affairs which I consulted are:

(1) 7(V)S, "General International Organization," pts. 4–8;
(2) 5475-E-40C, "Executive Committee of UN Preparatory Commission," pt. 1;
(3) 5475-J-40C, "Preparatory Commission of UN";
(4) 211-C. (S), "UN Security Council."

Reference is made in the book to three printed reports of the Department of External Affairs:

(1) *Report on the United Nations Conference on International Organization.* Conference series 1945, no. 2. Ottawa: King's Printer, 1947;
(2) *The United Nations 1946.* Conference series 1946, no. 3. Ottawa: King's Printer, 1947;
(3) *Documents on Canadian External Relations.* vol. 12, 1946. Ottawa: Supply and Services, 1977.

Two publications of the State Department of the United States have been used:

(1) *Foreign Relations of the United States, 1945.* Vol. 1. Washington: United States Government Printing Office, 1967;
(2) *Foreign Relations of the United States, 1946.* Vol. 1. Washington: United States Government Printing Office, 1974.

The publications which I cite are:

Acheson, Dean. *Present at the Creation*. New York: Norton, 1969.

Gladwyn, Lord. *The Memoirs of Lord Gladwyn*. London: Weidenfeld and Nicolson, 1972.

Hasluck, Paul.
"Twelve months on the Security Council." Address at the University of Western Australia on 9 September 1947.
Workshop of Security. Melbourne and London: F. W. Cheshire, 1948.
Diplomatic Witness, Australian Foreign Affairs 1941–1947. Melbourne: Melbourne University Press, 1980.

Martin, John Bartlow. *Adlai Stevenson of Illinois*. New York: Doubleday, 1976.

Vandenberg, Arthur H., Jr., ed. *The Private Papers of Senator Vandenberg*. Boston: Houghton Mifflin, 1952.

And finally, I wish to acknowledge the influence of Arnold Toynbee's *A Study of History*, (London: Oxford Univ. Press) on my writing and thought during the period covered by this book. I read the first three volumes of the collection in the late thirties and the next three in the early forties. In particular, Toynbee's influence pervades my essay of February 1946 (pp. 152–59), *An Approach to some of the Basic Problems of Foreign Policy*.

Notes

Chapter 1
 1. Percival Spear, *The Oxford History of Modern India, 1740–1975*, 2d edition (Delhi: Oxford University Press, 1978), p. 2.

Chapter 2
 1. *New York Times*, 28 March 1969.
 2. Department of External Affairs, *Statements and Speeches*, 47/6.

Chapter 3
 1. *Foreign Relations of the United States, 1945*, 1:671, 671, 753, 889. (Hereafter referred to as *FRUS 1945*.)
 2. *New York Times*, 28 March 1969.
 3. Arthur H. Vandenberg, Jr., ed., *The Private Papers of Senator Vandenberg*, p. 191.
 4. *FRUS 1945*, pp. 570–71.
 5. Ibid., p. 774.
 6. Ibid., p. 923.
 7. Ibid., p. 1331.
 8. Ibid., p. 1336.
 9. Paul Hasluck, "Twelve months on the Security Council," p. 1.
 10. Ibid., p. 2.
 11. *FRUS 1945*, p. 1073.
 12. Ibid., p. 1119.
 13. H. 271 of 3 June 1945, D.E.A. file 7(V) S, pt. 8.
 14. Gladwyn, *Memoirs*, p. 159.
 15. J. B. Martin, *Adlai Stevenson of Illinois*, p. 237.
 16. D.E.A. file 7(V)S, pt. 7.
 17. *FRUS 1945*, p. 1223.
 18. *Report on the United Nations Conference on International Organization*, Ottawa, 1945.
 19. *The United Nations 1946*, Ottawa, 1947.
 20. An amended version was included in the printed report of the Conference, pp. 35–36.

Chapter 4

1. The number of nations entitled to vote at the beginning of the San Francisco Conference was 46. Three countries were added at San Francisco: Argentina, Byelorussia, and the Ukraine. Denmark was added at the end of the Conference. Poland became a member of the Preparatory Commission, thus increasing the number of member nations to 51. The total number of possible votes in the Preparatory Commission was, however, 50 since Costa Rica did not send a delegation.

2. Hasluck, *Diplomatic Witness*, p. 229.

3. The printed official list of delegations is misleading. It shows as chief delegates a number of people who took little part in the Executive Committee. Thus L. B. Pearson of Canada was present for only about the first two weeks of the ten weeks the Executive Committee was in session and H. V. Evatt of Australia for only three weeks.

4. Gladwyn, *Memoirs*, p. 177.

5. Despatch no. 17 of 3 September 1945 entitled "The first fortnight." D.E.A. file 5475-E-40C, pt. 1.

6. *Foreign Relations of the United States, 1946*, 1:161. (Hereafter referred to as *FRUS 1946*.)

7. Extract from verbatim minutes.

8. Despatch no. 42 of 16 September 1945, D.E.A. file 5475-E-40C, pt. 1.

9. D.E.A. file 7 (V)S, pt. 4.

10. Hasluck, *Diplomatic Witness*, p. 230.

Chapter 5

1. Despatch no. 2 of 2 November 1945. D.E.A. file 5475-J-40C.

2. For China's views on 28 September 1945 see *FRUS 1945*, p. 1159. For the views of Chile and Brazil at the beginning of September see *FRUS 1945*, p. 1443.

3. Despatch no. 448 of 6 November 1945. D.E.A. file 5475-J-40C.

4. *FRUS 1945*, p. 1159.

5. Stettinius wrote in his memorandum of 23 August 1945,

The Secretary General should, if possible, not be a national of one of the Big Five; he should be chosen because of his qualifications. It is recommended that our first choice should be Mr. Norman A. Robertson, Under Secretary of State for External Affairs of Canada. Other possibilities are: Ambassador L. B. Pearson, Canada; Mr. Adrian Pelt, Netherlands; Mr. Stanley M. Bruce, Australia; Mr. D. D. Forsyth, South Africa; and Mr. C. Parra Perez, Venezuela. (Ibid., p. 1439).

On 24 December 1945 Adlai Stevenson reported that in a discussion of possible secretaries-general Gromyko had "suggested that it should not be a North American." (*FRUS 1945*, p. 1507.) Later Gromyko said that, while the Soviet Union had nothing against either a Canadian secretary-general or Pearson personally, with the headquarters in the United States it was unable to agree that the secretary-general should come from another American country. (*Documents on Canadian External Relations*, vol. 12, 1946, p. 629. See also p. 626.)

6. *FRUS 1945*, p. 1440.

7. Letter from Charles Ritchie to Hume Wrong, 27 March 1946, D.E.A. file 211-C.

8. Paul Hasluck, *Workshop of Security*, pp. 153–54.

9. Escott Reid, Memorandum of 28 December 1945 entitled "Comments on the Work of the Preparatory Commission," paragraph 19.

10. *FRUS 1945*, pp. 1439–40.

11. Dean Acheson, *Present at the Creation*, pp. 481, 598.

12. Hasluck, *Diplomatic Witness*, pp. 252, 258.

13. A slightly revised version of this memorandum of 28 December 1945 was sent to the Department of External Affairs on 14 January 1946. Both versions are in D.E.A. file 5475-J-40C.

Chapter 6

1. The extract printed here is in *Documents on Canadian External Relations*, 1946, p. 696. The memorandum and a memorandum of 1 October 1946 by an officer of the State Department commenting on it are in *FRUS 1946*, pp. 199–204.

2. *Documents on Canadian External Relations*, 1946, p. 632.

3. *FRUS 1945*, p. 1505.

4. Hasluck, *Diplomatic Witness*, p. 237.

Chapter 7

1. *FRUS 1945*, p. 1473.

2. *Report on the United Nations Conference on International Organization*, pp. 34–35.

3. Hasluck, *Workshop of Security*, pp. 63–64.

4. Despatch no. 21 of 26 November 1945 from the Canadian Delegation to the Preparatory Commission, D.E.A. file 5475-J-40C.

5. Telegram no. 11 of 27 November 1945 and undated memorandum by C. S. A. Ritchie attached to Escott Reid's letter of 26 October 1945 to Wrong, D.E.A. file 5475-J-40C.

6. Enclosure to letter from Escott Reid to Wrong of 2 October 1945, D.E.A. file 5475-J-40C.

7. Hasluck, *Workshop of Security*, pp. 62–66.

8. Hasluck, *Diplomatic Witness*, p. 267.

9. *Documents on Canadian External Relations*, vol. 12, 1946, p. 625.

10. Ibid., p. 628.

11. Hume Wrong's memorandum in its final form is published in *Documents on Canadian External Relations*, vol. 12, 1946, pp. 673–80. This volume contains on pp. 685–710 the memoranda I wrote for the guidance of the Canadian delegation to the U.N. General Assembly which met in New York in October 1946.

Index